Peter Christen Asbjørnsen

Fairy tales from the far North

Peter Christen Asbjørnsen

Fairy tales from the far North

ISBN/EAN: 9783743307513

Manufactured in Europe, USA, Canada, Australia, Japa

Cover: Foto ©ninafisch / pixelio.de

Manufactured and distributed by brebook publishing software (www.brebook.com)

Peter Christen Asbjørnsen

Fairy tales from the far North

CONTENTS

	Page
The Ram and the Pig who went into the Woods to live by Themselves	1
The Golden Bird	8
The Fox as Herdsboy	20
Ashiepattle, who ate with the Troll for a Wager	22
The Quern at the Bottom of the Sea	27
Little Butterkin	34
The Contrary-minded Woman	39
The Woodpecker	45
The Man's Daughter and the Woman's Daughter	47
The Hare who had been Married	58
The Squire's Bride	61
All Women are alike	69
One's own Children are always the Prettiest	77
Old Father Bruin in the Wolfpit	79
The Doll in the Grass	82
The Hen who went to Dovrefjeld to save the World	87
Squire Peter	91
Bird Dauntless	100
The Town Mouse and the Country Mouse	116
Soria Maria's Castle	122
Well Done, Ill Paid	138
Ashiepattle and his Goodly Crew	142
Gudbrand on the Hill-side	155
The Twelve Wild Ducks	162

Contents

	Page
The Bear and the Fox :	
1. Slip Pine-Root, Grip Fox-Foot	174
2. The Bear and the Fox make a Wager	175
3. The Bear and the Fox go into Partnership	176
4. Reynard wants to taste Horseflesh	180
The Cock who fell into the Brewing Vat	182
The Cock and the Fox	189
The Three Princesses in the Blue Mountain	192
The World's Reward	220
The Companion	226
Nanny who wouldn't go Home to Supper	246
The Lad with the Beer Keg	253
Little Fred and his Fiddle	259
The Storehouse Key in the Distaff	269
The Lad who went wooing the Daughter of old Mother Corner	272
The Princess whom nobody could silence	283
Farmer Weatherbeard	289

THE RAM
AND THE PIG
WHO WENT
INTO THE WOODS
TO LIVE
BY THEMSELVES

There was once upon a time a ram, who was being fattened up for killing. He had, therefore, plenty to eat, and he soon became round and fat with all the good things he got. One day the dairy-maid came, and gave him some more food.

"You must eat, ram," she

said; "you'll not be long here now, for to-morrow we are going to kill you."

"There's an old saying, that no one should sneer at old women's advice, and that advice and physic can be had for everything except death," thought the ram to himself; "but perhaps I might manage to escape it this time."

And so he went on eating till he was full, and when he was quite satisfied he ran his horns against the door, burst it open, and set off to the neighbouring farm. There he made straight for the pig-sty, to look for a pig with whom he had struck up an acquaintance on the common, since when they had always been good friends and got on well together.

"Good day, and thanks for your kindness last time we met," said the ram to the pig.

"Good day, and thanks to you," said the pig.

"Do you know why they make you so comfortable, and why they feed you and look after you so well?" said the ram.

"No," said the pig.

"There are many mouths to feed on this farm, you must know," said the ram; "they are going to kill you and eat you."

"Are they?" said the pig. "Well, much good may it do them!"

"If you are of the same mind as I, we will go into the woods and build a house and live by ourselves; there is nothing like having a home of your own, you know," said the ram.

Yes, the pig was quite willing. "It's nice to be in fine company," said he, and off they started.

When they had got a bit on the way they met a goose.

"Good day, my good people, and thanks for your kindness last time we met," said the goose. "Where are you off to?"

"Good day, and thanks to you," said the ram. "We had it altogether too comfortable at our place, so we are off to the woods to live by ourselves. In your own house you are your own master, you know," said he.

"Well, I'm very comfortable where I am," said the goose;

"but why shouldn't I join you? Good company makes the day shorter," said she.

"But neither hut nor house can be built by gabbling and quacking," said the pig. "What do you think you can do?"

"Good counsel and skill may do as much as a giant's will," said the goose. "I can pluck moss and stuff it into the crevices, so that the house will be warm and comfortable."

Well, she might come with them, thought the pig, for he liked the place to be warm and cosy.

When they had gone a bit on the way—the goose was not getting along very fast—they met a hare, who came scampering out of the wood.

"Good day, my good people, and thanks for your kindness the last time we met," said the hare. "How far are you going to-day?" said he.

"Good day, and thanks to you," said the ram; "we had it altogether too comfortable at our place, so we are off to the woods to build a house and live by ourselves. When you have tried both East and West, you'll find that a home of your own is after all the best," said he.

"Well, I have, of course, a house in every bush," said the hare; "but I have often said to myself in the winter, that if I lived till the summer I would build a house, so I have a good mind to go with you and build one after all," said he.

"Well, if the worst comes to the worst, we might take you with us to frighten the dogs away," said the pig, "for you couldn't help us to build the house, I should say."

"There is always something for willing hands to do in this world," said the hare. "I have teeth to gnaw pegs with, and I have paws to knock them into the walls, so I'll do very well for a carpenter; for 'good tools make good work,' as the man said, when he skinned his mare with an auger," said the hare.

Well, he might come with them and help to build the house; there could be no harm in that.

When they had got a bit further on the way, they met a cock.

"Good day, my good people, and thanks for your kindness last time we met," said the cock; "where are you all going to-day?" he said.

"Good day and thanks to you," said the ram; "we had it altogether too comfortable at our place, so we are off to the woods to build a house and live by ourselves. 'For unless at home you bake, you'll lose both fuel and cake,'" said he.

"Well, I am comfortable enough, where I am," said the cock, "but it's better to have your own roost than to sit on a stranger's perch and crow; and that cock is best off who has a home of his own," said he. "If I could join such fine company as yours, I too would like to go to the woods and build a house."

"Well, flapping and crowing is all very well for noise, but it won't cut joists," said the pig. "You can't help us to build a house," he said.

"It is not well to live in a house where there is neither dog nor cock," said the cock; "I am early to rise and early to crow."

"Yes, 'early to rise, makes one wealthy and wise,' so let him come with us!" said the pig. He was always the heaviest sleeper. "Sleep is a big thief, and steals half one's life," he said.

So they all set off to the woods and built the house. The pig felled the trees and the ram dragged them home; the hare was the carpenter, and gnawed pegs and hammered them into walls and roof; the goose plucked moss and stuffed it into the crevices between the logs; the cock crew and took care that they did not oversleep themselves in the mornings, and when the house was ready and the roof covered with birch-bark and thatched with turf, they could at least live by themselves, and they were all both happy and contented.

"It's pleasant to travel both East and West, but home is, after all, the best," said the ram.

But a bit further into the wood two wolves had their lair, and when they saw that a new house had been built hard by they wanted to know what sort of folks they had got for neighbours. For they thought, "a good neighbour is better than a brother in a

"SUCH TREATMENT I NEVER MET WITH BEFORE," SAID THE WOLF

foreign land, and it is better to live among good neighbours than to be known far and wide."

So one of them made it his business to call there and ask for a light for his pipe. The moment he came inside the door the ram rushed at him, and gave him such a butt with his horns that the wolf fell on his head into the hearth; the pig snapped and bit, the goose nipped and pecked, the cock flew up on a rafter and began to crow and cackle, and the hare became so frightened that he scampered and jumped about, both high and low, and knocked and scrambled about from one corner of the room to the other.

At last the wolf managed to get out of the house.

"Well, to know one's neighbours is to add to one's wisdom," said the wolf, who was waiting outside; "I suppose you had a grand reception, since you stayed so long. But what about the light? I don't see either pipe or smoke," said he.

"Yes, that was a nice light I got, and a nice lot of people they were," said he who had been inside. "Such treatment I never met with before, but 'as you make your bed so you must lie,' and 'an unexpected guest must put up with what he gets,'" said the wolf. "No sooner had I got inside the door, than the shoemaker threw his last at me, and I fell on my head in the middle of the forge; there sat two smiths, blowing bellows and pinching and snipping bits of flesh off me with red-hot tongs and pincers; the hunter rushed about the room looking for his gun, but as luck would have it, he couldn't find it. And up on the rafters sat some one beating his arms about and shouting: 'Let's hook him! let's hook him! Sling him up! sling him up!' and if he had only got hold of me I should never have got out alive."

THE GOLDEN BIRD

THERE was once upon a time a king who had a garden; in that garden there was an apple-tree, and on that apple-tree there grew a golden apple every year; but when the time came to pluck the apple, it was gone, and no one knew who took it or what became of it; but gone it was.

The king had three sons, and one day he told them that he who could bring him the apple, or get hold of the thief, should have the kingdom after him, no matter whether he was the eldest, the second or the younger son.

The eldest set out first and sat down under the tree to keep watch for the thief. Soon after dark a golden bird came flying and the light from it was so strong and dazzling, that it could be seen a long way off. When the prince saw the bird and the dazzling light, he became so frightened, that he dared not stay any longer, but rushed indoors as fast as he could.

Next morning the apple was gone; the prince had then, however, recovered his courage and began to get ready for his journey and wanted to set off to find the bird. The king fitted him out in grand style and spared neither money nor fine raiment. When the prince had gone a bit on the way he became hungry, opened his scrip and sat down to his breakfast by the road side. A fox then came out of the wood and sat down and looked at him.

"Do give me a little to eat," said the fox.

"I'll give you some powder and shot," said the prince; "my food I shall want myself; nobody can tell how far and how long I may have to travel," said he.

"Just so," said the fox, and so he went back into the wood again.

When the prince had finished his meal and rested awhile he set out on his way again. After a long time he came to a big city, and in that city there was an inn, where there was always joy and never any sorrow; he thought that would be a nice place to stop at, and so he remained. And there was such dancing and drinking and joy and merry-making, that he forgot the bird and his father and his journey and the whole kingdom.

Away he was and away he stopped.

The next year the second prince was to watch for the thief in the garden; he also sat down under the tree when the apple began to ripen. But one night, all of a sudden, the golden bird came flying, shining like the sun; the prince became so afraid that he took to his heels and ran indoors as fast as he could.

In the morning the apple was gone, but the prince had then recovered his courage and wanted to set out and find the bird. He began to get ready and the king fitted him out in grand style and spared neither money nor fine raiment. But the same thing happened to him as to his brother; when he had got a bit on the way he became hungry, opened his scrip and sat down to his breakfast by the roadside. A fox then came out from the pine wood and sat down and looked at him.

"Do give me a little to eat," said the fox.

"I'll give you some powder and shot," said the prince; "my food I shall want myself; nobody can tell how far and how long I may have to travel," said he.

"Just so," said the fox, and so he went back into the wood again.

When the prince had finished his meal and rested awhile, he set out on his way again. After a long time he came to the same city and the same inn, where there was always joy and never any sorrow; and there he also thought it would be nice to stop, and the first he met was his brother, and so he remained. The brother had been leading a gay and reckless life and had scarcely any clothes left on his back; but now he began afresh, and there was such dancing and drinking and joy and merriment that the second prince also forgot the bird and his father and his journey and the whole kingdom. Away he was and away he stopped.

When the time came for the apple to ripen again the youngest prince was to go into the garden and watch for the thief. He took a companion with him who was to help him up into the tree, and he also took with him a keg of beer and a pack of cards to pass away the time with so that he should not fall asleep. All of a sudden they saw a bright light, as if from the sun; every feather of the bird could be seen long before it came to the tree. The prince climbed up into the tree and at the same time the golden bird swooped down and took the apple; the prince tried to seize the bird, but he only caught a feather out of its tail.

So he went to the king's bedroom, and as he came in with the feather, it became as light as day.

He also wanted to try if he could find his brothers and catch the bird, for he had been so near to it that he had got a feather from its tail and would know it again anywhere, he said.

Well, the king went and pondered long whether he should let him go, for he thought the youngest would not fare any better than the two eldest, who ought to have more knowledge of the world, and he was afraid he should lose him also. But the prince begged so earnestly that at last he got permission to go.

He then began to get ready and the king fitted him out in grand style, both with clothes and money, and so he set off.

When he had travelled for some time he became hungry and took his scrip and sat down to have his breakfast, but just as he was in the midst of it, a fox came out of the wood and sat down close by his side and looked at him.

"Do give me a little to eat," said the fox.

"I shall want the food myself," said the prince, "for I cannot tell how far I shall have to travel, but I have enough to give you a little."

When the fox had got the piece of meat he asked the prince where he was going.

Yes, that he would tell him.

"If you will listen to me, I will help you, and you will have good luck," said the fox.

The prince promised he would, and so they set off together. They travelled a while till they came to the same city and the same inn, where there was always joy, but no sorrow.

"I must keep outside here; the dogs are rather a nuisance," said the fox, and so he told the prince where his brothers were to be found and what they were doing; "and if you go in there you will not get any further either," said he.

The prince promised he would not go in there, and gave him his hand on it, and so each went his way. But when the prince came to the inn and heard the noise and merriment going on he felt he must go in; there was no help for it, and when he met his brothers there was such rejoicing that he forgot both the fox and the journey and the bird, and his father. But when he had been there a while the fox came— he had ventured into the city after all—and opened the door a little and made a sign to the prince, saying that now they must be off. So the prince bethought himself, and they went their way.

When they had travelled a while they saw a big mountain far away. The fox said:

"Three hundred miles at the back of that mountain there is a gilded linden-tree with golden leaves, and in that tree sits the golden bird from which you took the feather."

Thither they travelled together. When the prince was going to catch the bird the fox gave him some bright feathers which he was to wave in his hands, and so attract the bird, which would then fly down and sit on his hand.

But the fox said he must not touch the linden-tree, for inside it was a big troll, who owned it, and if the prince only touched the smallest twig the troll would come out and kill him on the spot.

No, he would not touch it, said the prince; but when he had got the bird on his hand, he thought he must have a twig of the tree; there was no help for it, it was so bright and beautiful. So he took a tiny little sprig, but the same moment the troll came out.

"Who is that stealing my tree and my bird?" roared the troll, and he was so angry that he spurted sparks of fire.

"Thieves believe that all men steal," said the prince; "but only those get hanged who do not steal properly," said he.

The troll said that made no difference, and was going to kill him, but the prince begged him to spare his life.

"Well," said the troll, "if you can bring me back the horse which my nearest neighbour has taken from me, you will get off with your life."

"Where shall I find it, then?" said the prince.

"Oh, he lives three hundred miles at the back of that big blue mountain against the horizon yonder," said the troll.

The prince promised he would do his best. But when he came back to the fox he found him in rather a bad temper.

"Now you have got yourself into trouble," said the fox; "if

you had listened to me we could have been on our way home by this," said he.

So they had to make a fresh start, for the prince had pledged his word, and his life depended on his finding the horse.

At last they got there, but as the prince was going to take the horse the fox said:

"When you come into the stable you will find all sorts of bridles hanging on the wall, both of gold and silver; you must not touch them, for then the troll will come and kill you right away; you must take the ugliest and shabbiest you see."

Yes, the prince promised he would; but when he came into the stable he thought it was quite unreasonable not to take a fine bridle, for there were plenty of them, and so he took the brightest he could find. It was as bright as gold, but just then the troll came and was so angry that sparks flew from him.

"Who is that stealing my horse and my bridle?" he shrieked.

"Thieves believe that all men steal," said the prince; "but only those get hanged who do not steal properly," said he.

"Well, that makes no difference. I'll kill you on the spot," shouted the troll.

But the prince begged him to spare his life.

"Well," said the troll, "if you can bring me back the fair damsel which my nearest neighbour has taken from me I will spare you."

"Whereabouts does he live, then?" asked the prince.

"Oh, he lives three hundred miles at the back of that big blue mountain against the horizon yonder," said the troll.

The prince promised he would fetch the damsel, and was allowed to go, and so he escaped with his life.

But when he came out you may imagine how angry the fox was.

"Now you've got yourself into trouble again," said he; "if you had listened to me we could have been on our way home long ago. I almost think I will not go with you any further."

But the prince begged and prayed and promised he would never do anything else but what the fox told him, if he would only remain with him. At last the fox gave in, and they became firm friends again; so they set off once more and came at last to where the fair damsel was.

"Well," said the fox, "I have your promise, but I dare not let you in to the troll, after all; this time I must go myself." So he went in, and after a while he came out with the damsel, and so they went back the same way they had come.

When they got to the troll, who had the horse, they took both the horse and the brightest bridle; and when they got to the troll, who had the linden tree and the bird, they took both the tree and the bird and started off with them.

When they had got a bit on the way, they came to a field of rye, and the fox then said:

"I hear a thundering noise; you had better go on ahead; I will remain here a while," he said. He then plaited himself a gown of rye-straw, in which he looked like a preacher. All at once the three trolls came rushing along, hoping to overtake the prince.

"Have you seen any one passing here with a fair damsel, a horse with a golden bridle, a golden bird, and a gilded linden-tree?" they shouted to the fox, as he stood there preaching.

"Well, I've heard from my grandmother's grandmother, that something of the kind passed this way, but that was in the good old times, when my grandmother's grandmother baked halfpenny cakes and gave back the halfpenny."

Then all the trolls burst out laughing: "Ha, ha, ha!" they laughed and held on to one another.

"If we have slept so long, we may as well turn our noses homewards, and go to sleep again," they said, and so they went back the way they came.

The fox then set off after the prince, but when they came to the city, where the inn and his brothers were, he said:

"I dare not go through the town on account of the dogs; I must

"HA, HA, HA!" THE TROLLS LAUGHED, AND HELD ON TO ONE ANOTHER

go my own way just above here, but you must take good care your brothers do not get hold of you."

But when the prince came into the city, he thought it would be too bad if he did not look in upon his brothers and have a word with them, and so he tarried there for a while.

When the brothers saw him, they came out and took both the damsel, and the horse, and the bird, and the linden-tree, and everything from him, and they put him in a barrel, and threw him into the sea; and so they set off home to the king's palace, with the damsel, and the horse, and the bird, and the linden-tree, and everything. But the damsel would not speak, and she became pale and wretched to look upon; the horse got so thin and miserable that it could hardly hang together; the bird became silent and shone no more, and the linden-tree withered.

In the meantime the fox was sneaking about outside the city, where the inn and the merriment were, and was waiting for the prince and the damsel, and wondered why they did not return.

He went hither and thither, waiting and watching for them, and at last he came down to the shore, and when he saw the barrel, which was lying out at sea drifting, he shouted: "Why are you drifting about there, you empty barrel?"

"Oh, it is I," said the prince in the barrel.

The fox them swam out to sea as fast as he could, got hold of the barrel, and towed it to land; then he began to gnaw the hoops, and when he had got some off the barrel, he said to the prince: "Stamp and kick."

The prince stamped and kicked till all the staves flew about, and out he jumped from the barrel.

So they went together to the king's palace, and when they got there the damsel regained her beauty and began to talk, the horse became so fat and sleek that every hair glistened; the light shone from the bird and it began to sing; the linden-tree began to blossom and its leaves to sparkle, and the damsel said, "He is the one who has saved us."

18   THE GOLDEN BIRD

They planted the linden-tree in the garden, and the youngest prince was to marry the princess, for such the damsel really was; but the two eldest brothers were put each in a spiked barrel and rolled down a high mountain.

Then they began to prepare for the wedding, but the fox first

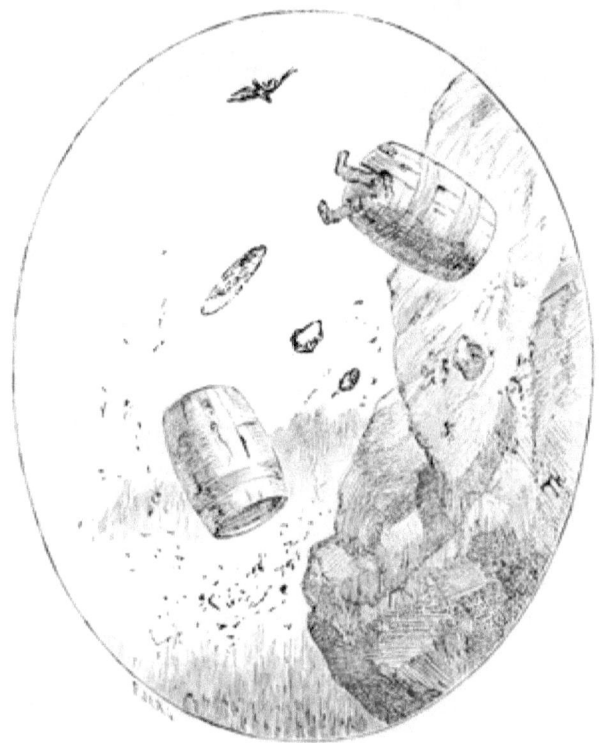

THE TWO ELDEST BROTHERS WERE PUT EACH IN A SPIKED BARREL
AND ROLLED DOWN A MOUNTAIN.

asked the prince to put him on the block and cut his head off, and although the prince both prayed and cried, there was no help for it; he would have to do it. But as he cut the head off, the fox turned into a handsome prince, and he was the brother of the princess, whom they had rescued from the troll.

So the wedding came off and everything was so grand and splendid, that the news of the festivities reached all the way here.

THE FOX AS HERDSBOY

There was once upon a time a woman, who went out to look for a herdsboy, and so she met a bear.

"Where are you going?" said the bear.

"Oh, I'm looking for a herdsboy," answered the woman.

"Won't you take me?" asked the bear.

"Well, if you only knew how to call the flock," said the wife. "Ho-y!" shouted the bear.

"No, I won't have you!" said the woman, when she heard this, and went on her way.

When she had gone on a while, she met a wolf.

"Where are you going?" said the wolf.

"I am looking for a herdsboy," said the woman.

"Won't you take me?" said the wolf.

THE FOX AS HERDSBOY

"Well, if you only knew how to call the flock," said the woman. "U-g-h!" howled the wolf.

"No, I won't have you," said the woman.

When she had gone a bit further, she met a fox.

"Where are you going?" said the fox.

"Oh, I'm looking for a herdsboy," said the woman.

"Won't you take me?" asked the fox.

"Well, if you only knew how to call the flock," said the woman.

"Dil-dal-holom!" called the fox in a thin, squeaky voice.

"Yes, I'll take you for a herdsboy," said the woman; and so she put the fox to look after her flocks. On the first day he ate up all the goats belonging to the woman; the second day he finished all her sheep, and the third day he ate all the cows. When he came home in the evening, the woman asked what he had done with all the flocks.

"The skulls are in the brook and the bones in the wood," said the fox.

The woman was busy churning, but she thought she might as well go and look for her flocks. While she was away, the fox slipped into the churn and ate all the cream. When the woman came back and saw this, she became so angry, that she took a small clot of cream, which was left, and threw it after the fox, splashing the end of his tail with it, and that's the reason why the fox has a white tip to his tail!

ASHIEPATTLE* WHO ATE WITH THE TROLL FOR A WAGER

THERE was once upon a time a peasant who had three sons. He was badly off, and old and feeble, and the sons would not do any work.

To the farm belonged a large pine forest, and the father wanted his sons to cut timber in it, and try to get some of his debts paid off. At last he got them to listen to him, and the eldest one was to go out first and fell trees. When he got into the forest and began felling an old bearded pine, a great big troll came up to him.

"If you cut down my trees, I'll kill you!" said the troll.

When the lad heard this, he threw down the axe and set off home as fast as he could. He got there quite out of breath, and told what had happened to him, but the father said he was chicken-hearted; the trolls had never frightened him from felling trees when he was young, he said.

The next day the second son was to go, and the same thing happened to him. He had no sooner struck some blows at the pine than the troll came and said:

"If you cut down my trees, I'll kill you!"

The lad hardly dared to look at him; he threw down the axe and took to his heels, just like his brother, only rather quicker.

---

* The favourite hero of most Norwegian fairy tales is called *Askeladen*, a sort of male Cinderella and is always the youngest son of the family.

"IF YOU DON'T BE QUIET," SHOUTED THE LAD TO THE TROLL, "I'LL SQUEEZE YOU
JUST AS I SQUEEZE THE WATER OUT OF THIS STONE."

When he came home the father became angry, and said that the trolls had never frightened him when he was young.

On the third day Ashiepattle wanted to set out.

"You indeed!" said the two eldest; "you'll never be able to do anything, you who have never been outside the door!"

Ashiepattle did not answer, but only asked for plenty of food to take with him. His mother had nothing ready, and so she put on the pot and made a cheese for him, which he placed in his scrip, and then set out from home. When he had been felling trees awhile, the troll came to him and said:

"If you cut down my trees, I'll kill you!"

But the lad was not slow; he ran into the forest for the cheese and squeezed it, so that the whey spurted from it.

"If you don't be quiet," he shouted to the troll, "I'll squeeze you just as I squeeze the water out of this white stone."

"Oh dear, oh dear! do spare me!" said the troll, "and I'll help you."

Well, on that condition the lad would spare him, and as the troll was clever at felling trees, they cut them down by the dozen during the day. Towards evening the troll said:

"You had better come home with me; it is nearer than to your place."

Well, the boy went home with him, and when they got there the troll was to light the fire on the hearth, while the boy fetched the water for the porridge. But the two iron buckets that were there were so big and heavy he was not even able to move them. So the boy said:

"It is hardly worth while to take these thimbles with me; I'll go and fetch the whole well."

"Oh dear, no!" said the troll, "I cannot lose my well; you make the fire, and I'll fetch the water."

When he came back with the water, they boiled a great big cauldron of porridge.

"If it's all the same to you," said the lad, "I'll lay a wager I'll eat more than you."

"All right," said the troll, for he thought he could easily manage that; but the boy took his scrip without the troll seeing it, and tied it in front of him, and managed to put more porridge in the scrip than he ate himself. When the scrip was full he took his knife and cut a slit in it.

The troll looked at him, but didn't say anything. When they had been eating a good while the troll put away his spoon, and said:

"I can't eat any more."

"You must eat," answered the lad. "I'm scarcely half-way through. Do as I did, and cut a hole in your stomach, and then you can eat as much as you like."

"But I suppose it hurts one dreadfully?" asked the troll.

"Oh, nothing worth talking about," answered the lad.

So the troll did as the lad told him, and as you will easily understand, that was the end of him. But the lad took all the silver and gold which was in the mountain, and went home. With that he would be able to pay off something of his father's debt.

THE QUERN AT THE BOTTOM OF THE SEA

Once upon a time in the old, old days there were two brothers, one of whom was rich and the other poor. When Christmas Eve came the poor brother had not a morsel in the house, neither of meat nor bread; and so he went to his rich brother, and asked for a trifle for Christmas, in heaven's name. It was not the first time the brother had helped him, but he was always very close-fisted, and was not particularly glad to see him this time.

"If you'll do what I tell you, you shall have a whole ham," he said. The poor brother promised he would, and was very grateful into the bargain.

"There it is, and now go to the devil!" said the rich brother, and threw the ham across to him.

"Well, what I have promised I must keep," said the other one. He took the ham, and set out. He walked and walked the whole day, and as it was getting dark he came to a place where the lights were shining brightly. "This is most likely the place," thought the man with the ham.

In the wood-shed stood an old man with a long white beard, cutting firewood for Christmas.

"Good evening," said he with the ham.

"Good evening to you," said the man. "Where are you going so late?"

"I am going to the devil—that is to say, if I am on the right way," answered the poor man.

"Yes, you are quite right; this is his place," said the old man. "When you get in, they will all want to buy your ham, for ham is scarce food here; but you must not sell it unless you get the hand-quern, which stands just behind the door. When you come out again, I'll teach you how to use it. You will find it useful in many ways."

The man with the ham thanked him for all the information, and knocked at the door.

When he got in, it happened just as the old man had said. All the imps, both big and small, flocked around him like ants in a field, and the one outbid the other for the ham.

"Well," said the man, "my good woman and I were to have it for Christmas Eve, but since you want it so badly I will let you have it. But if I am going to part with it, I want that hand-quern which stands behind the door."

The devil did not like to part with it, and higgled and haggled with the man, but he stuck to what he had said, and in the end the devil had to part with the quern.

When the man came out, he asked the old wood-cutter how

he was to use the quern, and when he had learned this, he thanked the old man and set out homewards as quickly as he could; but after all he did not get home till the clock struck twelve on Christmas Eve.

"Where in all the world have you been?" said his wife. "Here have I been sitting, hour after hour, waiting and watching for you, and have not had as much as two chips to lay under the porridge pot."

"Well, I couldn't get back before;" said the man. "I have had a good many things to look after, and I've had a long way to walk as well; but now I'll show you something," said he and put the quern on the table. He asked it first to grind candles, then a cloth, and then food and beer, and everything else that was good for Christmas cheer; and as he spoke the quern brought them forth. The woman crossed herself time after time and wanted to know where her husband had got the quern from; but this he would not tell her.

"It does not matter where I got it from; you see the quern is good and the mill stream is not likely to freeze," said the man. So he ground food and drink and all good things during Christmas; and the third day he invited his friends, as he wanted to give them a feast. When the rich brother saw all that was in the house, he became both angry and furious, for he begrudged his brother everything.

"On Christmas Eve he was so needy that he came to me and asked for a trifle in heaven's name; and now he gives a feast, as if he were both a count and a king," said the brother. "Where did you get all your riches from?" he said to his brother.

"From just behind the door," he answered, for he did not care to tell his brother much about it. But later in the evening, when he had drank a little freely, he could no longer resist, but brought out the quern.

"There you see that which has brought me all my riches," he said, and so he let the quern grind first one thing and then another.

When the brother saw this, he was determined to have the quern at all cost, and at last it was settled he should have it, but three hundred dollars was to be the price of it. The brother was, however, to keep it till the harvest began; "for if I keep it so long, I can grind out food for many years to come," he thought.

During that time you may be sure the quern did not rust, and when the harvest began the rich brother got it; but the other had taken great care not to show him how to use it.

It was evening when the rich brother got the quern home, and in the morning he asked his wife to go out and help the haymakers; he would get the breakfast ready himself to-day, he said.

When it was near breakfast time he put the quern on the breakfast table.

"Grind herrings and broth, and do it quickly and well," said the man, and the quern began to bring forth herrings and broth, and filled first all the dishes and tubs, and afterwards began flooding the whole kitchen.

The man fiddled and fumbled and tried to stop the quern, but however much he twisted and fingered it, the quern went on grinding, and in a little while the broth reached so high that the man was very near drowning. He then pulled open the parlour door, but it was not long before the quern had filled the parlour also, and it was just in the very nick of time that the man put his hand down into the broth and got hold of the latch, and when he had got the door open, he was soon out of the parlour, you may be sure. He rushed out, and the herrings and the broth came pouring out after him, like a stream, down the fields and meadows.

The wife, who was out haymaking, now thought it took too long a time to get the breakfast ready.

"If my husband doesn't call us soon, we must go home whether or no: I don't suppose he knows much about making broth, so I must go and help him," said the wife to the haymakers.

They began walking homewards, but when they had got a bit up the hill they met the stream of broth with the herrings tossing about in it and the man himself running in front of it all.

"I wish all of you had a hundred stomachs each!" shouted the man; "but take care you don't get drowned." And he rushed past them as if the Evil One was at his heels, down to where his

THE MAN RUSHED OUT OF THE HOUSE, AND THE HERRINGS AND THE BROTH CAME POURING OUT
AFTER HIM LIKE A STREAM

brother lived. He asked him for heaven's sake to take back the quern, and that at once; "If it goes on grinding another hour the whole parish will perish in broth and herrings," he said. But the brother would not take it back on any account before his brother had paid him three hundred dollars more, and this he had to do. The poor brother now had plenty of money, and before long he bought a farm much grander than the one on which his rich brother lived, and with the quern he ground so much gold that he covered the farmstead with gold plates and, as it lay close to the shore, it glittered and shone far out at sea. All those who sailed past wanted to call and visit the rich man in the golden house, and everybody wanted to see the wonderful quern, for its fame had spread both far and wide, and there was no one who had not heard it spoken of.

After a long while there came a skipper who wanted to see the quern; he asked if it could grind salt. Yes, that it could, said he who owned it; and when the skipper heard this he wanted the quern by hook or by crook, cost what it might, for if he had it he thought he need not sail far away across dangerous seas for cargoes of salt.

At first the man did not want to part with it, but the skipper both begged and prayed, and at last he sold it and got many, many thousand dollars for it.

As soon as the skipper had got the quern on his back he did not stop long, for he was afraid the man would change his mind, and as for asking how to use it he had no time to do that; he made for his ship as quickly as he could, and when he had got out to sea a bit he had the quern brought up on deck.

"Grind salt, and that both quickly and well," said the skipper, and the quern began to grind out salt so that it spurted to all sides.

When the skipper had got the ship filled he wanted to stop the quern, but however much he tried and whatever he did the quern went on grinding, and the mound of salt grew higher and higher, and at last the ship sank.

There at the bottom of the sea stands the quern grinding till this very day, and that is the reason why the sea is salt.

C

LITTLE BUTTERKIN

Once upon a time there was a woman who was sitting baking. She had a little boy who was so fat and plump and who was so fond of good food that she called him Butterkin. She also had a dog called Goldtooth.

One day, all of a sudden, the dog began to bark.

"Run out, Butterkin!" said the woman, "and see what Goldtooth is barking at."

So the boy ran out and came back, saying:

"Oh, mother, mother! There's a great big troll-wife coming here, with her head under her arm and a bag on her back."

"Run under the table and hide yourself," said his mother.

The big troll-wife then came in.

"Good day!" she said.

"Good day to you!" said Butterkin's mother.

"Is Butterkin at home to-day?" asked the troll-wife.

"No, he is in the forest with his father, after the ptarmigan," answered the woman.

"That's a pity," said the troll; "for I have such a nice little silver knife I wanted to give him."

"Peep, peep, here I am," said Butterkin under the table, and crept out.

"I am so old and stiff in my back," said the troll, "you must get into the bag and find it yourself."

No sooner was Butterkin in the bag than the troll threw it across her back and walked off with him. When they had gone a bit on the way the troll got tired and asked:

"How far have I to go before I can lie down and sleep?"

"About a mile," answered Butterkin. The troll then put down the bag by the roadside and went in among the bushes by herself and lay down to sleep. In the meantime Butterkin took the opportunity, pulled out his knife, cut a hole in the bag and jumped out; he then put a big root of a fir-tree in his place and ran home to his mother. When the troll-wife reached home and saw what she had in the bag she flew into a great rage.

The next day the woman sat baking again. All at once the dog began to bark.

"Run out, Butterkin," said she, "and see what Goldtooth is barking at."

"Oh, mother, mother! It's that terrible old troll!" said Butterkin. "Here she is again, with her head under her arm and a big bag on her back."

"Run under the table and hide yourself," said his mother.

"Good-day!" said the troll-wife. "Is Butterkin at home to-day?"

"No, indeed he is not," said his mother; "he is out in the forest with his father, after the ptarmigan."

"That's a pity!" said the troll; "for I have such a nice little silver fork I wanted to give him."

"Peep, peep! Here I am!" said Butterkin, and crept out.

"I am so stiff in my back," said the troll, "you must get into the bag and find it yourself."

No sooner was Butterkin in the bag than the troll threw it across her back and walked off with him. When they had gone a good bit on the way the troll got tired and asked:

"How far have I to go before I can lie down and sleep?"

"About two miles," answered Butterkin. The troll then put down the bag by the roadside and went into the wood and lay down to sleep. While the troll-wife took her nap, Butterkin cut a hole in the bag, and when he had got out he put a big stone in his place. As soon as the troll-wife reached home she lighted a great fire in the hearth and put on a large cauldron in which to boil Butterkin, but when she took the bag to empty Butterkin into the cauldron, the stone fell out, and knocked a hole in the bottom of the cauldron, so the water rushed out and put out the fire. The troll then became very angry and said:

"Let him make himself ever so heavy, I'll be even with him yet."

The third time it happened just as before; Goldtooth began to bark and so the mother said to Butterkin:

"Run out, Butterkin, and see what Goldtooth is barking at."

Butterkin then ran out and came back saying:

"Oh, mother, mother! It's that troll again, with her head under her arm and a bag on her back."

"Run under the table and hide yourself," said the mother.

"Good day!" said the troll, as she came in through the door. "Is Butterkin home to-day?"

"No, indeed he is not," said his mother; "he is in the forest with his father, after the ptarmigan."

"That's a pity!' said the troll-wife, "for I have such a nice little silver spoon I wanted to give him."

"Peep, peep! Here I am!" said Butterkin and crept out from under the table.

"I am so stiff in my back," said the troll, "you must get into the bag and find it yourself."

No sooner had Butterkin got into the bag than the troll threw it across her back and walked away with it.

This time the troll-wife did not lie down and sleep, but went straight home with Butterkin in the bag. It was a Sunday when they got home, and so the troll said to her daughter:

"Now you must take Butterkin and kill him and make broth of him, till I come back again, for I am going to church, and shall ask some friends for dinner."

When she was gone, the daughter went to take Butterkin to kill him, but she did not quite know how to set about it.

"Wait a bit! I'll show you how to do it!" said Butterkin; "just put your head on the block and see how it's done."

She did so, poor silly thing, and Butterkin took the axe and cut off her head, just as if it had been that of a chicken; he then put the head in the bed and the body in the cauldron, and made broth of the daughter, and when he had done this he climbed up on the roof, just over the door, taking with him the fir-root and the stone, and put the first over the door and the other across the top of the chimney.

When the people came home from church and saw the head in the bed, they thought that the daughter had lain down and was asleep, so they thought they would taste the broth.

"This Butterkin-broth tastes nice!" said the troll-wife.

"This daughter-broth tastes nice!" said Butterkin, but they took no heed.

The troll-wife then took the spoon to taste the broth.

"This Butterkin-broth tastes nice," she said.

"This daughter-broth tastes nice," said Butterkin down the chimney.

They then began to wonder who it could be, and went out to see. But when they came outside the door, Butterkin threw the fir-root and stone at their heads and killed them all on the spot. He then took all the gold and silver that was in the house, and you may imagine how rich he became; and so he went home to his mother.

THE CONTRARY WOMAN

There was once upon a time a man who had a wife, and she was so contrary and cross-grained that it was not an easy thing at all to get on with her. The husband fared worst of all; whatever he was for, she was always against.

So it happened one Sunday in summer that the man and the woman went out to see how the crops looked.

When they came to a corn-field on the other side of the river the man said:

"It's ready for reaping; to-morrow we must begin."

"Yes, to-morrow we can begin and clip it," said the woman.

"What is it you say? Are we going to clip it? Are we supposed not to reap corn any longer?" said the man.

"No, it must be clipped," said the woman.

"There is nothing so dangerous as a little knowledge," said the man; "one would think you had lost what little sense you had! Have you ever seen anybody clipping corn?" said he.

"Little I know, and less I want to know," said the woman; "but this I do know, that the corn shall be clipped and not reaped." There was no use talking any more about that; clipped it should be.

So they walked on wrangling and quarrelling, till they came to the bridge across the river, close to a deep pool.

"There's an old saying," said the man, "that good tools make good work; I fancy that'll be a queer harvest which is cut with a pair of shears," said he. "Shall we not settle to reap the corn, after all?"

"No, no! it must be clipped, clipped, clipped!" shouted the woman jumping up and clipping her fingers under the man's nose.

In her passion she forgot to look where she was going, and all at once she stumbled over one of the beams on the bridge and fell into the river.

"Old habits are hard to change," thought the man, "but it would be a wonder if I, for once, got my way."

He waded out into the pool and got hold of her by the hair, till her head was just out of the water.

"Shall we reap the corn then?" he said.

"Clip, clip, clip!" screamed the woman.

"I'll teach you to clip," thought the man, and ducked her under the water. But that wasn't of much use; "they must clip it," she said, as he brought her to the surface again.

"I do believe the woman is crazy," said the man to himself; "many are mad and don't know it, and many have sense and don't use it; but I must try once more, anyhow," said he. But no sooner had he ducked her under again than she held her hand above the water and began to clip with her fingers, like a pair of shears. Then the man got furious and kept her under so long that her hand all of a sudden fell under water, and the woman became so heavy that he had to let go his hold.

"NO, NO! IT MUST BE CLIPPED, CLIPPED, CLIPPED!" SHOUTED THE WOMAN, CLIPPING HER FINGERS UNDER THE MAN'S NOSE.

"If you want to drag me down into the pool with you, you may lie there, you wretch!" said the man. And so the woman was drowned.

But after a while he thought it wasn't right that she should lie there and not be buried in Christian soil, so he went along the river and searched and dragged for her; but for all his searching

SHE HELD HER HAND ABOVE THE WATER AND BEGAN TO CLIP WITH HER FINGERS, LIKE A PAIR OF SHEARS

and all his dragging he could not find her. He took the people on the farm and others in the neighbourhood with him, and they began dragging the river all the way down; but for all the searching they could not find the woman.

"Well," said the man, "this is not much use! This woman was a sort by herself; while she was alive she was altogether a contrary one, and it is not likely she'll be different now," he said, "we must search up the river for her, and try above the fall; perhaps she has floated upwards."

So they went up the river and searched and dragged for her above the fall, and there, sure enough, she lay. That shows what a contrary woman she was!

THE WOODPECKER

In those days when the saints used to wander about on earth, St. Peter once came to a woman who was sitting baking oatcakes. Her name was Gertrude, and she had a red cap on her head.

As St. Peter had been walking a long distance and was hungry, he asked her for a bit of her cake. Yes, he might have some, and she took a tiny lump of dough and began to roll it out; but it became so big that it filled the whole of the board. No, that cake was too big, he shouldn't have that one.

She then took a still smaller lump of dough, but when she had rolled it out and put it on the slab to bake, that one also became too big. He shouldn't have that one either.

The third time she took a still smaller lump, a tiny little one; but this time also the cake became too big.

"I have nothing to give you," said the woman; "you may as well go without your bit, for all the cakes are too big."

Then St. Peter became angry and said: "Because you begrudge me such a trifle you shall be punished, and you shall become a bird and seek your food between the bark and the wood and have nothing to drink except when it rains."

He had no sooner said the last word than she became a woodpecker and flew from the hearth up the chimney. To this day you can see her flying about with her red cap on and her body all over black from the chimney. She is always tapping and pecking at the trees for food, and piping when it is going to rain, for she is always thirsty and is then waiting for water.

THE MAN'S DAUGHTER AND THE WOMAN'S DAUGHTER

ONCE upon a time there were a man and a woman who got married; they had each a daughter. The woman's daughter was lazy and idle and would never do any work, and the man's daughter was active and willing, but for all that, she could never please the stepmother, and both the woman and her daughter would have liked to get rid of her.

One day they were sitting by the well spinning; the woman's daughter had flax to spin, but the man's daughter had nothing else but bristles.

"You are always so clever and smart," said the woman's daughter, "but still I'm not afraid to try and see who can spin the most."

They agreed, that the one whose thread first broke, should be put into the well.

All at once the man's daughter's thread broke, so she was put into the well. But when she came to the bottom she found she was not hurt; and far and wide around she saw nothing but a beautiful green meadow.

She walked for some time in the meadow, till she came to a hedge which she had to climb over.

"Do not step heavily on me," said the hedge, " and I'll help you another time." She made herself as light as a feather and stepped over so carefully that she scarcely touched it.

So she went on a bit farther, till she came to a brindled cow, which had a milk pail on her horns; it was a fine large cow, and her udder was round and full of milk.

"Please do milk me," said the cow, "for I am so full of milk; drink as much as you like and pour the rest over my hoofs, and I'll help you some other time."

The man's daughter did as the cow had asked her; the moment she took hold of the teats the milk squirted into the pail, then she drank as much as she could and the rest she poured over the cow's hoofs, and the pail she hung on the horns again.

When she had gone a bit further she met a large ram, which had such long thick wool that it trailed along the ground, and on one of his horns hung a large pair of shears.

"Please do shear me," said the ram, "for here I have to go about panting with all this wool, and it is so warm I am almost stifled. Take as much wool as you like and twist the rest round my neck, and I'll help you another time."

She was quite willing, and the ram lay down in her lap; he was so quiet and she sheared him so neatly, that she did not make a single scratch in his skin. She then took as much as she wanted of the wool, and the rest she twisted round the ram's neck.

A little further on she came to an apple-tree, which was so laden with apples that all the branches were bent to the ground. Close to the trunk stood a small pole.

"Please do pluck some of my apples," said the tree, "so that my branches can straighten themselves, for it is quite painful to stand so crooked, but be sure and strike me gently and lightly, so that you do not injure me. Eat as many as you like and place the rest around my root, and I'll help you some other time."

So she plucked all she could reach, and then she took the pole and carefully knocked down all the other apples; she ate till she was satisfied, and the rest she placed neatly round the root.

Then she walked on a long, long way, till she came to a large

SHE WENT IN TO THE TROLL-WIFE AND ASKED IF THEY WANTED
A SERVING MAID

farm, where a troll-wife and her daughter lived. She went in and asked if they wanted a serving maid.

"Oh, it's no use," said the troll-wife, "we have tried many, but none of them were good for anything." But she begged so hard, that at last they took her into service; and the troll-wife gave her a sieve and told her to fetch some water in it. She thought it was rather unreasonable that they should ask her to fetch water in a sieve, but she went all the same, and when she came to the well the little birds were singing:

> "Rub in clay!
> Put in hay!
> Rub in clay!
> Put in hay!"

She did so and was then able to carry the water in the sieve easily enough, but when she came home with the water and the troll-wife saw the sieve, she said:

"You have not done that by yourself."

The troll-wife then told her to go into the cow-house and clean it out and then milk the cows; but when she came there she found that the shovel was so big and heavy she could not use it, she could not even lift it. She did not know what to do, but the birds sang to her that she should take the handle of the besom and throw a little out with it and then all the rest would follow.

She did this and no sooner had she done it than the cow-house was as clean as if it had been cleaned and swept. She had next to milk the cows, but they were so restless and kicked and plunged so that she could not get any milking done at all. Then she heard the birds singing outside:

> "A little squirt!
> A little sip!
> To little birds!"

She squirted a little milk out to the birds and then all the cows stood still and let her milk them; they neither kicked nor plunged, they did not even lift a leg.

When the troll-wife saw her coming in with the milk she said:

"You have not done this by yourself. Now you must take this black wool and wash it white."

The girl did not know how she should get this done, for she had never seen any one who could wash black wool white. But she said nothing, she took the wool and went to the well with it. The little birds sang to her that she should take the wool and put it in the big bucket that was standing near the well, and it would become white.

"Oh dear, oh dear!" said the troll-wife, when the girl came in with the wool. "It's no use keeping you, you can do everything; you will worry the life out of me in the end, it is better you should go your way."

The troll-wife then brought out three caskets, a red, a green, and a blue one, and the girl might take whichever she liked, and that was to be her wages. She did not know which one to take, but the little birds sang:

> "Take not the green!
> Take not the red!
> But take the blue!
> On which we've put
> Three little crosses!"

She then took the blue one, as the birds had told her.

"A curse upon you," said the troll-wife, "you will be sure to suffer for this."

When the man's daughter was going the troll-wife threw a red-hot iron bar after her, but the girl ran behind the door and hid herself, so the bar missed her, for the little birds had told her what to do.

She set off as quickly as she could; but when she came to the apple tree she heard a rumbling noise behind her on the road; it was the troll-wife and her daughter, who were after her. The girl got so frightened she did not know what to do with herself.

"Come here to me," said the apple-tree, "and I'll help you.

Hide yourself under my branches, for if they get hold of you, they will take the casket from you and tear you to pieces." The girl did so, and just then up came the troll-wife and her daughter.

"Have you seen any girl go past here?" said the troll-wife.

"Oh, yes," said the tree, "one ran past awhile ago; but she is now so far away you'll never overtake her."

The troll-wife then turned about and set off home.

The girl walked on a bit; but when she came to the ram, she heard the rumbling noise again on the road, and she became so frightened and terrified, that she did not know what to do with herself; for she knew it was the troll-wife who had changed her mind.

"Come here and I'll help you," said the ram. "Hide yourself under my wool and they won't see you; or else they'll take the casket from you and tear you to pieces."

All at once the troll-wife came rushing up.

"Have you seen a girl go past here?" she asked the ram.

"Oh, yes," said the ram, "I saw one a while ago, but she ran so fast that you will never overtake her." So the troll-wife turned round and went home.

When the girl had got as far as the cow, she heard the rumbling noise again on the road.

"Come here," said the cow, "and I'll help you; hide yourself under my udder, or else the troll-wife will take the casket from you, and tear you to pieces." Before long she came.

"Have you seen any girl go past here?" said the troll-wife to the cow.

"Yes, I saw one a while ago, but she is far away now, for she was running so fast that you will never overtake her," said the cow. The troll-wife then turned round and went home again.

When the girl had got a long long bit on the way and was not far from the hedge, she heard the noise again on the road; she became terribly frightened, for she knew it was the troll-wife who had come back again.

"Come here and I'll help you," said the hedge, "creep in

among my twigs, and they won't see you; or else they will take the casket from you and tear you to pieces." She made haste to hide herself among the twigs of the hedge.

"Have you seen any girl go past here?" said the troll-wife to the hedge.

"No, I have not seen any girl," said the hedge, and it became so angry you could hear it crackle. Then it made itself so big, it was no use trying to get over it. There was no help for it; the troll-wife had to turn round and go home again.

When the man's daughter got home both the woman and her daughter were still more spiteful than they had been before; for now she was still more beautiful, and so grand, that it was a pleasure to look at her. She was not allowed to stop with them, but they sent her to the pig-sty, where she was to live. She then began to wash and clean out the place, and then she opened her casket to see what she had got for wages; when she opened it she found there was so much gold and silver, and so many beautiful things in it, that both the walls and roof were covered, and the pig-sty became more magnificent than the finest palace.

When the step-mother and the daughter saw this they were quite beside themselves, and began to ask her what sort of service she had been in.

"Oh," she said, "you can easily guess since I have had such wages. Such a mistress to work for, and such people you will not easily find!"

The woman's daughter then wanted to set out and go into service, so that she also might get such a golden casket.

They then sat down to spin again; but this time the woman's daughter was to spin bristles, and the man's daughter flax, and the one who first broke the thread would be put into the well.

Before long the woman's daughter broke her thread, as you may guess, and so they threw her into the well.

Everything happened as before; she fell to the bottom, but did not hurt herself, and then she came to a beautiful green meadow. When she had walked a bit she came to the hedge.

"Do not step heavily on me, and I will help you another time," said the hedge.

"Oh, what do I care about a lot of twigs," she said, and trod heavily on the hedge, so that it groaned.

In a little while she came to the cow, which wanted milking again.

"Please do milk me," said the cow, "and I will help you another time; drink as much as you like, and pour the rest over my hoofs."

This she did; she milked the cow, and drank as long as she was able, till there was nothing left to pour over the hoofs. She then threw the pail down the hill and went her way. When she had gone a bit further she came to the ram, which was going about trailing his wool along the ground.

"Do shear me, and I'll help you another time," said the ram; "take as much of the wool as you like, but twist the rest around my neck." She did this, but sheared the ram so roughly that she made big gashes in his skin; and then she took all the wool away with her.

In a little while she came to the apple-tree, which was quite bent down under the weight of its apples.

"Please do pluck my apples, so that my branches can straighten themselves, for it is painful to stand so crooked," said the apple-tree, "but be careful not to injure me; eat as many as you like, but place the rest at my root, and I'll help you another time."

She plucked some of the nearest, and those she could not reach she knocked down with the pole; but she did not care how she did it. She tore down large branches, and ate till she was unable to eat any more; and then she threw the rest under the tree.

When she had walked a little way she came to the farm, where the troll-wife lived, and asked to be taken into service. The troll-wife said she would not have any servant girl, for either they were good for nothing or else they were far too clever, and cheated her of what she had. The woman's daughter did not give in, but said she must have a place; and then the troll-wife said she would take her, if she was good for anything.

The first thing she got to do was to fetch water in the sieve. She went to the well and poured water into the sieve, but as fast as she poured it in it ran out. The birds then sang:

> "Rub in clay!
> Put in hay!
> Rub in clay!
> Put in hay!"

But she didn't take any notice of what the bird's sang; she threw the clay at them, so that they flew away, and she had to go back with an empty sieve, and got scolded by the troll-wife. She was then to clean out the cow-house and milk the cows, but she thought she was too good for that. She went into the cow-house, however; and when she got there she found she could not use the shovel; it was so big. The birds said the same to her as to the man's daughter—that she should take the besom and sweep out the litter, and all the rest would follow; but she took the besom and threw it at the birds. When she was going to milk the cows they were so restless that they kicked and plunged. and every time she had got a little in the pail they kicked it over. The birds sang:

> "A little squirt!
> A little sip!
> For little birds!"

But she struck and beat the cows, flung and threw everything she could get hold of at the birds, and carried on in a way that was never heard of. She had not, of course, cleaned the cow-house or milked the cows, so when she came in she got both blows and scolding from the troll-wife. She was then to wash the black wool white, but she did not fare any better with that. The troll-wife thought this was too bad, and so she brought out three caskets—one red, one green, and one blue—and told her she had no use for her, as she was fit for nothing; but she should have a casket all the same for her wages, and could choose which she liked best. Then the birds sang:

> "Take not the green!
> Take not the red!
> But take the blue!
> Which we have put
> Three crosses on!"

She did not take any notice of what the birds sang, but took the red one, which was the gaudiest. So she set out on her way home, and got there without any trouble, for there was no one in pursuit of her.

When she got home the mother was greatly rejoiced to see her, and they went at once into the parlour and placed the casket there, for they thought there was nothing but gold and silver in it, and they believed that both the walls and the roof would be covered with gold. But as soon as they opened the casket there swarmed out of it vipers and toads, and when the daughter opened her mouth it was just the same; vipers and toads and all sorts of vermin fell out, till at last it was impossible to live in the same house with her. And that was all she got for serving the troll-wife!

THE HARE WHO HAD BEEN MARRIED

Once upon a time a hare was running and frisking about in a cornfield.

"Hurray! hurrah! hurray!" he shouted, as he jumped and skipped along.

All of a sudden he turned a somersault, and found himself standing on his hind legs in a new-sown cornfield.

Just then a fox came slinking by.

"Good day, good day to you!" said the hare. "I feel so jolly to-day, for I have been married, you must know!"

"That's a good thing for you," said the fox.

"Oh, I don't know so much about that," said the hare, "for she was rather a cross-grained creature, and she turned out a regular scold of a wife, she did."

"That was a bad thing for you," said the fox.

"Oh, it wasn't so bad," said the hare, "for I got a lot of money with her, and she had a house of her own besides."

"That was a very good thing indeed," said the fox.

"Oh, I don't know so much about that," said the hare, "for the house got burnt down, and everything we had along with it."

"That was really too bad," said the fox.

"Oh, not so very bad after all," said the hare, "for that cross-grained wife of mine was burnt as well."

"HURRAY! HURRAY! HURRAY!" SHOUTED THE HARE, AS HE JUMPED AND SKIPPED ALONG.

THE SQUIRE'S BRIDE

ONCE upon a time there was a rich squire who owned a large farm, and had plenty of silver at the bottom of his chest and money in the bank besides; but he felt there was something wanting, for he was a widower.

One day the daughter of a neighbouring farmer was working for him in the hayfield. The squire saw her and liked her very much, and as she was the child of poor parents he thought, if he only hinted that he wanted her, she would be ready to marry him at once.

So he told her he had been thinking of getting married again.

"Ay! one may think of many things," said the girl, laughing slyly. In her opinion the old fellow ought to be thinking of something that behoved him better than getting married.

"Well, you see, I thought that you should be my wife!"

"No, thank you all the same," said she, "that's not at all likely."

The squire was not accustomed to be gainsaid, and the more she refused him the more determined he was to get her.

But as he made no progress in her favour, he sent for her father and told him that if he could arrange the matter with his daughter he would forgive him the money he had lent him, and he would also give him the piece of land which lay close to his meadow into the bargain.

"Yes, you may be sure I'll bring my daughter to her senses," said the father. "She is only a child, and she doesn't know what's best for her." But all his coaxing and talking did not help matters. She would not have the squire, she said, if he sat buried in gold up to his ears.

The squire waited day after day, but at last he became so angry and impatient that he told the father, if he expected him to stand by his promise, he would have to put his foot down and settle the matter now, for he would not wait any longer.

The man knew no other way out of it, but to let the squire get everything ready for the wedding; and when the parson and the wedding guests had arrived the squire should send for the girl as if she were wanted for some work on the farm. When she arrived she would have to be married right away, so that she would have no time to think it over.

The squire thought this was well and good and so he began brewing and baking and getting ready for the wedding in grand style. When the guests had arrived the squire called one of his farm lads and told him to run down to his neighbour and ask him to send him what he had promised.

"But if you are not back in a twinkling," he said shaking his fist at him, "I'll——"

He did not say more, for the lad ran off as if he had been shot at.

"My master has sent me to ask for that you promised him," said the lad, when he got to the neighbour, "but there is no time to be lost, for he is terribly busy to-day."

THE BOY RODE HOME ON THE BAY MARE AT FULL GALLOP

"Yes, yes! Run down into the meadow and take her with you. There she goes!" answered the neighbour.

The lad ran off and when he came to the meadow he found the daughter there raking the hay.

"I am to fetch what your father has promised my master," said the lad.

"Ah, ha!" thought she. "Is that what they are up to?"
"Ah, indeed!" she said. "I suppose it's that little bay mare

SOME PULLED AT THE HEAD AND THE FORE LEGS OF THE MARE AND OTHERS PUSHED BEHIND

of ours. You had better go and take her. She stands there tethered on the other side of the pease-field," said the girl.

The boy jumped on the back of the bay mare and rode home at full gallop.

"Have you got her with you?" asked the squire.

"She is down at the door," said the lad.

"Take her up to the room my mother had," said the squire.

"But, master, how can that be managed?" said the lad.

"You must just do as I tell you," said the squire. "If you cannot manage her alone you must get the men to help you," for he thought the girl might turn obstreperous.

When the lad saw his master's face he knew it would be no use to gainsay him. So he went and got all the farm-tenants who were there to help him. Some pulled at the head and the fore legs of the mare and others pushed from behind, and at last they got her up the stairs and into the room. There lay all the wedding finery ready.

"Now, that's done, master!" said the lad; "but it was a terrible job. It was the worst I have ever had here on the farm."

"Never mind, you shall not have done it for nothing," said his master. "Now send the women up to dress her."

"But I say, master——!" said the lad.

"None of your talk!" said the squire. "Tell them they must dress her and mind and not forget either wreath or crown."

The lad ran into the kitchen.

"Look here, lasses," he said; "you must go upstairs and dress up the bay mare as bride. I expect the master wants to give the guests a laugh."

The women dressed the bay mare in everything that was there, and then the lad went and told his master that now she was ready dressed, with wreath and crown and all.

"Very well, bring her down!" said the squire. "I will receive her myself at the door," said he.

There was a terrible clatter on the stairs; for that bride, you know, had no silken shoes on.

E

When the door was opened and the squire's bride entered the parlour you can imagine there was a good deal of tittering and grinning.

And as for the squire you may be sure he had had enough of that bride, and they say he never went courting again.

THE DOOR OPENED AND THE SQUIRE'S BRIDE ENTERED THE PARLOUR

ALL WOMEN ARE ALIKE

Once upon a time a man and a woman were going to sow, but they had no seed-corn and no money to buy any with either. They had only one cow and this the man was to go to town with and sell to get money for the seed-corn.

But when the time came the wife would not let the man go, for she was afraid he would spend the money on drink. So she set off herself with the cow and took with her a hen as well.

Close to the town she met a butcher.

"Are you going to sell that cow, mother?" he asked.

"Yes, that I am," she said.

"How much do you want for it then?"

"I suppose I must have a shilling for the cow, but the hen you can have for two pounds," she said.

"Well," said the butcher, "I haven't any use for the hen, and you can easily get rid of that when you get to the town, but I'll give you a shilling for the cow."

She sold the cow and got her shilling, but nobody in the town would give two pounds for a tough, old hen. So she went back to the butcher and said:

"I can't get rid of this hen, father. You'll have to take that as well since you took the cow."

"We'll soon settle that," said the butcher, and asked her to sit down. He gave her something to eat and so much brandy to drink that she became tipsy and lost her wits. While she slept it off the butcher dipped her into a barrel of tar and then put her in a heap of feathers.

When she woke up she found that she was feathered all over and she began to wonder: "Is it me? or is it not me? It must be a strange bird! But what shall I do to find out whether it is me, or whether it is'nt me? Now I know—if the calves will lick me and the dog doesn't bark at me, when I get home, then it is me."

The dog no sooner saw such a monster than it began barking with all its might as if there were thieves and vagabonds about the place.

"No, surely, it cannot be me," she said.

When she came to the cowhouse the calves would not lick her, because they smelt the tar.

"No, it cannot be me; it must be a strange bird," she said; and then she climbed up on top of the storehouse and began to flap with her arms as if she had wings and wanted to fly. When the man saw this he came out with his rifle and took aim at her.

"Don't shoot, don't shoot," cried his wife; "it is me."

"Is it you?" said the man. "Then don't stand there like a goat, but come down and tell me what you have been about."

She climbed down again, but found she had not a single penny left, for the shilling she got from the butcher she had lost while she was tipsy.

When the man heard this he said: "You are more mad than ever you were," and he became so angry that he said he would go away from everything and never come back if he did not find three women who were just as mad.

He set out and when he had got a bit on the way he saw a woman running in and out of a newly-built hut with an empty sieve. Every time she ran in she threw her apron over the sieve, as if she had something it, and then she turned it over on the floor.

WHEN THE MAN SAW THE STRANGE FIGURE ON THE ROOF HE CAME OUT WITH HIS RIFLE AND TOOK AIM AT IT

"What are you doing that for, mother?" asked he.

"Oh, I only want to carry in a little sun," she answered; "but I don't know how it is—when I am outside I have the sun in the sieve, but when I get inside I have lost it. When I was in my old hut I had plenty of sun, although I never carried in any. If any one could get me some sun I'd willingly give him three hundred dollars."

"Have you an axe?" said the man, "and I'll soon get you some sun."

He got an axe and cut out the openings for the windows which the carpenters had forgotten to do. The sun shone into the room at once and he got his three hundred dollars.

"That was one of them!" thought the man, and set out again.

In a while he came to a house where there was a terrible screaming and shouting going on. He went in and saw a woman, who was beating her husband on the head with a bat; and over his head she had pulled a shirt in which there was no hole for the neck.

"Do you want to kill your husband, mother?" he asked.

"No," she said, "I only want to make a hole for the neck in his shirt."

The man moaned and groaned and said: "Oh dear, oh dear! I pity those who have to try on new shirts. If any one could teach my wife how to make the hole for the neck in a different way, I'd willingly give him three hundred dollars."

"I'll soon do that," said the man; "only let me have a pair of scissors."

He got a pair and cut the hole, and then he took his money and went his way.

"That was the second of them!" he said to himself.

After a long while he came to a farm, where he thought he would rest awhile, so he went in.

"Where do you come from?" asked the woman.

"I come from Ringerige,"* answered the man.

* A district in the south of Norway.

"Oh dear, oh dear! are you from Himmerige?* Then you must know Peter, my second husband, poor soul!" said the woman. She had been married three times; the first and the last husbands were bad men, so she thought that the second, who had been a good husband, was the only one likely to go to heaven.

"Yes, I know him well," said the man.

"How is it with him there?" asked the woman.

"Oh, things are rather bad with him," said the man. "He knocks about from place to place, and has neither food nor clothes to his back, and as for money——"

"Goodness gracious!" cried the woman, "there's no need that he should go about in such a plight—he that left so much behind him. Here is a large loft full of clothes, which belonged to him, as well as a big chest of money. If you'll take it all with you you shall have the horse and trap to take it in; and he can keep both horse and trap, so that he can drive about from place to place; for he has no need to walk, I'm sure."

The man got a whole cartload of clothes and a chest full of bright silver dollars, and as much food and drink as he wanted. When he had finished he got into the trap and drove off.

"That's the third of them!" he said to himself.

But the woman's third husband was over in a field ploughing, and when he saw a stranger driving off with the horse and trap, he went home and asked his wife who it was who drove away with the horse.

"Oh," she said, "that was a man from heaven; he said that Peter, my second, poor dear soul, is so badly off that he walks about there from place to place, and has neither clothes nor money; so I sent him all his old clothes, which have been hanging here ever since, and the old money chest with the silver dollars."

The man understood at once what all this meant, and saddled a horse and set off at full gallop.

* "Himmerige," the Norwegian word for "heaven." The similarity between the two words "Himmerige" and "Kingerige" will easily explain the mistake made by the woman.

Before long he was close behind the man in the trap; who when he discovered he was pursued, drove the horse and trap into a thick part of the wood, pulled a handful of hair out of the horse's tail, and sprang up a hill, where he tied the horse's hair to a birch-tree, and lay down on his back under it, gaping and staring up into the clouds.

"Oh dear, oh dear, oh dear!" he said, as if talking to himself, when the woman's third husband came riding up; "well, I've never seen anything so wonderful! I've never seen the like of it!"

The husband stopped and looked at him for a while and wondered if the man was crazy, or what he was up to. At last he asked him:

"What are you staring at?"

"Well, I never saw the like!" exclaimed the man. "I've just seen some one driving straight into heaven, horse and all! There, you see part of the horse's tail hanging on the birch tree, and up among the clouds you can see the horse."

The husband looked up at the clouds and then at him and said:

"I don't see anything but the horse-hair on the birch-tree."

"No, of course you can't see it, where you stand," said the man, "but come and lie down here and look straight up; you must not take your eyes away from the clouds."

While the husband lay staring into the sky till the water ran from his eyes, the man jumped on the horse and set off, both with that and the horse and trap.

When the husband heard the rumbling noise on the road, he jumped up, but was so bewildered because the man had gone off with his horses that he did not think of setting after him till it was too late. He did not feel very proud, as you can imagine, when he came home to his wife, and when she asked him what he had done with the horse he said:

"Oh, I told the man he could take that with him as well to Peter, for I did not think it was right that he should jolt about in a trap up there; now he can sell the trap and buy a carriage."

"Oh, thank you for that! never did I think you were such a kind husband," said the woman.

When the man who had got the six hundred dollars and the cartload of clothes and money, came home, he saw that all the fields were ploughed and sown. The first thing he asked his wife was, where she had got the seed-corn from.

"Oh," said she, "I have always heard, that he who sows something gets something. So I sowed the salt which the carrier left here the other day, and if we only get rain soon, I think it will grow up nicely."

"Mad you are, and mad you'll be as long as you live," said the man; "but it doesn't much matter, for the others are no better than you."

ONE'S OWN CHILDREN ARE ALWAYS THE PRETTIEST

Once upon a time a man went out shooting in a forest, and there he met a woodcock.

"Pray, don't shoot my children," said the woodcock.

"What are your children like?" asked the man.

"Mine are the prettiest children in the forest," answered the woodcock.

"I suppose I mustn't shoot them then," said the man.

When he came back he carried in his hand a whole string of young woodcocks which he had shot.

"Oh dear, oh dear! Why, you have shot my children after all!" said the woodcock.

"Are these yours?" said the man. "Why, I shot the ugliest I could find."

"Yes, yes," answered the woodcock; "but don't you know that every one thinks one's own children the prettiest?"

OLD FATHER BRUIN IN THE WOLF-PIT

THERE was once upon a time a man who lived far away in the wood. He had many sheep and goats, but he could never keep the wolf away from them.

"I'll be even with you yet, Master Greylegs," he said at last, and began to dig a pit for the wolf. When he had dug it deep enough he placed a pole in the middle of the pit and on the top of the pole he fixed a board, and on the board he put a little dog. He then placed some twigs and branches across the pit, and on top of all he sprinkled some snow, so that the wolf should not see there was a trap underneath. When the night came the little dog got tired of being there.

"Bow-wow-wow!" it barked at the moon.

A fox just then came slinking along, and thought here was a fine chance. He made a spring and fell plump into the pit.

As the night wore on the little dog became so weary and hungry that it began to whine and bark.

"Bow-wow-wow," it barked.

All at once a wolf came slouching along. He thought here is a fat little morsel, and sprang plump into the pit.

Early in the grey morning the North wind began to blow and it became so cold that the little dog shivered and trembled, and was so weary and hungry.

"Bow-wow-wow-wow," it went on barking all the time.

A bear then came trudging along, and thought here was a nice tit-bit early in the morning; so he stepped out on the branches and fell plump into the pit.

As the morning wore on there came an old beggarwoman who was tramping about from place to place with a bag on her back. When she saw the little dog standing there barking she thought she would go and see if any animals had been caught in the trap during the night. She went down on her knees and peered into the pit.

"So you have been caught, Master Reynard, have you?" she said to the fox, for she saw him first; "serve you right, you old hen-thief. And you are there too, are you, Master Greylegs?" said she to the wolf. "Well, you have killed goats and sheep enough in your time, and now you'll suffer for it and get what you deserve. Hulloa, Father Bruin, are you in this nice little parlour too, you old horse-thief? We will cut you up and flay you, we will, and your skull we will nail up on the cow-house," shouted the woman excitedly, and shook her fists at the bear; but just then her bag slipped forward over her head, and the woman tumbled plump into the pit. There they sat staring at one another, all four of them, each in their corner—the fox in one, the wolf in the other, the bear in the third, and the old woman in the fourth.

When it became full daylight Reynard began to shake himself and whisk about, for he thought he might as well try to get out; but the old woman said:

"Can't you sit quiet, you old roost-robber, and not go frisking and trailing about in this way? Look at old Father Bruin; he sits as quiet as a parson in his study;" for she thought she had better make friends with the bear.

Then came the man who had set the trap for the wolf. First of all he dragged up the old woman, and then he killed all the animals; he spared neither old Father Bruin, nor Greylegs, nor Reynard, the hen-thief. The man thought he had made a good haul that night.

THE DOLL IN THE GRASS

Once upon a time there was a king who had twelve sons. When they were grown up he told them they must go out into the world and find themselves wives, who must all be able to spin and weave and make a shirt in one day, else he would not have them for daughters-in-law. He gave each of his sons a horse and a new suit of armour, and so they set out in the world to look for wives.

When they had travelled a bit on the way they said they would not take Ashiepattle with them, for he was good for nothing. Ashiepattle must stop behind; there was no help for it. He did not know what he should do or which way he should turn; he became so sad that he got off the horse and sat down on the grass and began to cry.

When he had sat awhile, one of the tussocks among the grass began to move, and out of it came a small white figure; as it came nearer, Ashiepattle saw that it was a beautiful little girl, but she was so tiny, so very, very tiny.

She went up to him and asked him if he would come below and pay a visit to the doll in the grass.

Yes, that he would; and so he did. When he came down below, the doll in the grass was sitting in a chair dressed very finely and looking still more beautiful. She asked Ashiepattle where he was going and what was his errand.

A SMALL WHITE FIGURE CAME OUT OF ONE OF THE TUSSOCKS AMONG THE GRASS

He told her they were twelve brothers, and that the king had given them each a horse and a suit of armour, and told them to go out in the world and find themselves wives, but that they must all be able to spin and weave and make a shirt in a day.

"If you can do that and will become my wife, I will not travel any further," said Ashiepattle to the doll in the grass.

Yes, that she would, and she set to work at once to get the shirt spun, woven and made; but it was so tiny, so very, very tiny, no bigger than—so!

Ashiepattle then returned home, taking the shirt with him; but when he brought it out, he felt very shy because it was so small. But the king said he could have her for all that, and you can imagine how happy and joyful Ashiepattle became.

The road did not seem long to him, as he set out to fetch his little sweetheart. When he came to the doll in the grass, he wanted her to sit with him on his horse, but no, that she wouldn't; she said she would sit and drive in a silver spoon, and she had two small white horses which would draw her. So they set out, he on his horse and she in the silver spoon; and the horses which drew her were two small white mice.

Ashiepattle always kept to one side of the road, for he was so afraid he should ride over her; she was so very, very tiny.

When they had travelled a bit on the way, they came to a large lake; there Ashiepattle's horse took fright and shied over to the other side of the road, and upset the spoon, so that the doll in the grass fell into the water. Ashiepattle became very sad, for he did not know how he should get her out again; but after a while a merman brought her up. But now she had become just as big as any other grown up being and was much more beautiful than she was before. So he placed her in front of him on the horse and rode home.

When Ashiepattle got there, all his brothers had also returned, each with a sweetheart; but they were so ugly and ill-favoured and bad-tempered, that they had come to blows with their sweethearts on their way home. On their heads they had hats which were painted with tar and soot, and this had run from their hats down their faces, so that they were still uglier and more ill-favoured to behold.

When the brothers saw Ashiepattle's sweetheart, they all became envious of him, but the king was so pleased with Ashiepattle and his sweetheart, that he drove all the others away, and so Ashiepattle was married to the doll in the grass; and afterwards they lived happy and comfortable for a long, long while; and if they are not dead, they must be still alive.

THE HEN WHO WENT TO DOVRE-FJELD TO SAVE THE WORLD

There was once upon a time a hen, which flew up in an oak-tree and perched there for the night. Before long she dreamt, that if she did not go to Dovrefjeld, the world would come to an end. All of a sudden she jumped down and set out on the road.

When she had gone a bit she met a cock.

"Good-day, Cocky Locky!" said the hen.

"Good-day, Henny Penny! where are you going so early?" said the cock.

"Oh, I am going to Dovrefjeld, so that the world shan't come to an end," said the hen.

"Who told you that, Henny Penny?" said the cock.

"I sat in the oak and dreamt it last night," said the hen.

"I'll go with you," said the cock. So they went a long way, till they met a duck.

"Good-day, Ducky Lucky!" said the cock.

"Good-day, Cocky Locky! where are you going so early?" said the duck.

"I am going to Dovrefjeld, so that the world shan't come to an end," said the cock.

"Who told you that, Cocky Locky?"

"Henny Penny!" said the cock.

"Who told you that, Henny Penny?" said the duck.

"I sat in the oak and dreamt it last night," said the hen.

"I'll go with you!" said the duck. So they set off and walked a bit, till they met a gander.

"Good-day, Gandy Pandy!" said the duck.

"Good-day, Ducky Lucky!" said the gander. "Where are you going so early?"

"I am going to Dovrefjeld, so that the world shan't come to an end," said the duck.

"Who told you that, Ducky Lucky?" said the gander.

"Cocky Locky!"

"Who told you that, Cocky Locky?"

"Henny Penny!"

"How do you know that, Henny Penny?" said the gander.

"I sat in the oak and dreamt it last night, Gandy Pandy," said the hen.

"I'll go with you!" said the gander. When they had gone on a bit, they met a fox.

"Good-day, Foxy Woxy!" said the gander.

"Good-day, Gandy Pandy!"

"Where are you going, Foxy Woxy?"

"Where are you going, Gandy Pandy?"

"I'm going to Dovrefjeld, so that the world shan't come to an end," said the gander.

"Who told you that, Gandy Pandy?" said the fox.

"Ducky Lucky!"

"Who told you that, Ducky Lucky?"

"Cocky Locky!"

"Who told you that, Cocky Locky?"

"Henny Penny!"

"How do you know that, Henny Penny?"

"I sat in the oak and dreamt last night that if we don't go to Dovrefjeld the world will come to an end," said the hen.

"Oh, nonsense!" said the fox, "the world won't come to an end if you don't get there. No, come home with me to my den; that's much better, for there it is cosy and comfortable."

So they followed the fox home to his den, and when they came there, the fox put so much wood on the fire that they all became sleepy; the duck and the gander settled in a corner, but the cock and the hen perched on a pole. As soon as the gander and the duck were asleep the fox seized the gander and put it on the fire and roasted it. The hen thought she smelt something burning, she jumped up to a higher perch and said half asleep:

"Faugh! How it stinks here!"

"Oh, nonsense," said the fox, "it is only the smoke coming down the chimney; go to sleep and shut your mouth." So the hen went to sleep. No sooner had the fox eaten the gander than he seized the duck; he took it and put it on the fire and roasted it and then set about to eat it. The hen then woke up again and flew up to a still higher perch.

"Faugh! How it stinks here," she said, and when she opened her eyes and saw that the fox had eaten both the gander and the duck, she flew up to the highest perch and settled there and looked up through the chimney.

"Just look at all the fine geese flying over there!" she said to the fox.

Reynard ran out, thinking to find another fat roast. In the meantime the hen woke up the cock and told him what had happened to Gandy Pandy and Ducky Lucky.

So Cocky Locky and Henny Penny flew up through the chimney, and if they hadn't got to Dovrefjeld the world would surely have come to an end!

SQUIRE PETER

There was once upon a time a poor couple who had nothing in the world but three sons. What the two eldest were called I don't know, but the youngest was called Peter.

When the parents died the children were to have all they left behind; but there was nothing but a porridge pot, a gridiron and a cat. The eldest, who was to have the best, took the pot.

"Every time I lend the pot I shall get the scrapings," he said.

The second took the gridiron.

"For when I lend it I shall get a bit to taste," said he.

But there was no choice for the youngest; if he wanted anything he would have to take the cat.

"If I lend the cat to any one I shall get nothing for it," he said; "if the cat gets a little milk she'll want it herself, but I'll take her with me any how; it's a pity she should be left behind to pine."

So the brothers set out into the world to try their fortune, and each went his own way. When the youngest had gone awhile the cat said:

"You'll not be sorry you didn't leave me behind. I'll now go into the forest and fetch some fine animal which you must take to the king's palace you see yonder, and say to the king you have come with a small present for him. When he asks who it is from you must say it is from Squire Peter."

Peter had not long to wait before the cat came back with a reindeer from the forest; she had jumped upon its head and when she had settled herself between its horns she said: "If you don't go straight to the king's palace I shall scratch your eyes out." The reindeer dared not do otherwise.

When Peter came to the palace he went into the kitchen with the reindeer and said:

"I have come with a small present for the king, which I hope he will accept."

The king came out into the kitchen and when he saw the fine big reindeer he was much pleased.

"But, dear friend! who is it that sends me such a fine present?" said the king.

"Oh, it's Squire Peter!" said the lad.

"Squire Peter!" said the king. "Ah, let me see, where is it he lives?" for he thought it was a shame he should not know such a worthy man.

But the lad would not tell him. He dared not for his master, he said.

So the king gave Peter some money and asked him to give his master his greetings and many thanks for the present.

THE KING CAME OUT INTO THE KITCHEN AND WHEN HE SAW THE ONE BIG REINDEER HE WAS MUCH PLEASED

The next day the cat went into the forest again and jumped up on the head of a stag, settled herself between its eyes and compelled it to go to the palace. Peter again went into the kitchen with it and said he came with a small present for the king if he would accept it. The king was still more pleased with the stag than with the reindeer, and asked again who it was that had sent him such a fine present.

"Oh, it's Squire Peter," said the lad; but when the king wanted to know where Squire Peter lived he got the same answer as the day before. This time he gave Peter still more money.

The third day the cat brought an elk. When Peter came into the kitchen at the palace, he said that he had a small present for the king if he would accept it. The king came out at once into the kitchen, and when he saw the fine, big elk he became so pleased he did not know which leg to stand upon. That time he gave Peter much more money; it must have been a hundred dollars.

The king was now most anxious to know where Squire Peter lived and began questioning him backwards and forwards, but the lad said he dared not tell him, for his master had given him strict orders not to disclose it.

"Well, ask Squire Peter to pay me a visit then," said the king.

Yes, he would do that, said the lad, but when he came out of the palace and met the cat, Peter said:

"You have got me into a fine scrape; the king now says I must visit him and I have nothing but the rags I walk in."

"Oh, don't trouble about that," said the cat. "In three days you shall have coach and horses, and fine clothes with gold trimmings and hangings, and then you can surely visit the king. But whatever you see at the palace you must say you have grander and finer things at home; you must not forget that."

No, he would be sure to remember, said Peter.

When the three days were over the cat came with the coach and horses and clothes and everything that Peter wanted; all was so grand that no one had seen anything like it before. So Peter set out for the palace and the cat ran alongside him.

The king received him well, but whatever he offered him and whatever he showed him Peter said it was all very well, but he had everything finer and grander at home. The king was not over pleased at this; but Peter went on just the same and at last the king became so angry that he could no longer contain himself.

"I'll go home with you," said the king, "and see if it is true that you have everything so much grander and finer; but if you have not told the truth it will be the worse for you. I'll say no more!"

"You have got me into a fine scrape this time," said Peter to the cat; "the king now wants to go home with me, but it will not be an easy thing to find my home."

"Oh, don't trouble about that," said the cat, "I will run on in front, and you need only follow me."

So they set off. Peter followed the cat, who ran on in front, and then came the king with all his suite. When they had driven a good bit on the way, they came to a large flock of fine sheep; the wool was so long it almost reached to the ground.

"If you will say that the sheep belong to Squire Peter when the king asks, you shall have this silver spoon," said the cat to the herdsboy. She had taken the spoon with her from the palace. Yes, he would willingly do that, said the herdsboy.

When the king came by, he said:

"I've never seen such a fine flock of sheep! To whom do they belong, my little boy?"

"Oh, they belong to Squire Peter," said the boy.

In a little while they came to a great big herd of fine brindled cows; they were so fat that their hides glistened.

"If you will say the cattle belong to Squire Peter when the king asks, you shall have this silver ladle," said the cat to the cow-girl. The silver ladle she had also taken with her from the palace.

"Yes, that I will," said the girl. When the king came up, he was quite surprised at the fine big cattle, for such a herd he thought he had never seen before; and so he asked the girl to whom those brindled cows belonged.

"Oh, they are Squire Peter's!" said the girl.

So they travelled on again, and then they came to a great big drove of horses. They were the finest one could see, big and sleek, and six of each colour, both brown and red, and cream-coloured.

"If you will say those horses belong to Squire Peter when the king asks, I'll give you this silver goblet," said the cat to the boy. The goblet she had also taken from the palace.

THEY THEN CAME TO A GREAT BIG DROVE OF HORSES

"Yes, that I will," said the boy. When the king came by, he became quite dazed at the fine drove of horses, for he had never seen the like of such horses, he said. He then asked the boy to whom those brown, red, and cream-coloured horses belonged.

"Oh, they are Squire Peter's!" said the boy.

When they had travelled a long, long way, they came to a castle. First there was a gateway of brass, then one of silver, and then one of gold. The castle itself was of silver, and glistened so brightly that it made one's eyes smart, for the sun was shining full upon it when they arrived.

They entered, and the cat told Peter to say he lived there. Inside the castle was still more splendid than outside; everything was of gold, both chairs and tables and benches. When the king had been round and seen it all from top to bottom, he became quite confounded.

"Yes, Squire Peter is much grander than I; there is no use denying that," he said; and then he wanted to return home. But Peter asked him to stop and sup with him, which the king agreed to; but he was cross and peevish the whole time. While they sat at table the troll, who owned the castle, came and knocked at the gate.

"Who eats my food and drinks my mead in there?" he cried. As soon as the cat heard him, she ran to the gate.

"Wait a little, and I'll tell you how the farmer gets his winter rye," said the cat. "First he ploughs his field, and then he manures it, and then he ploughs it again"; and so the cat went on till the sun rose.

"Just look behind at that beautiful damsel!" said the cat to the troll. The troll then turned round, and when he saw the sun he burst.

"All this is now yours," said the cat to Squire Peter. "And now you must cut my head off; it is the only thing I ask for all I have done for you."

"No," said Squire Peter, "that I will not do."

"You must," said the cat, "or I'll scratch your eyes out."

Squire Peter was then obliged to do it, although he was very loath. He cut the cat's head off, and the same moment she became the most beautiful princess any one could set eyes on, and Squire Peter fell in love with her then and there.

"All this splendour has formerly been mine," said the princess, "but the troll got me into his power and turned me into a cat, and ever since I have been at your parents'. You must now do as you like about making me your queen, for you are king over the whole realm," said the princess.

Squire Peter was, of course, only too glad to make her his queen. So the wedding took place, and the feasting lasted for eight days. And as I did not stay any longer with the squire and his queen I cannot tell you any more about them.

BIRD DAUNTLESS

ONCE upon a time there was a king who had twelve daughters, and he loved them so much that he never allowed them out of his sight; but every day after dinner, while the king slept, the princesses went out for a walk. Once, when the king was having his afternoon nap, the princesses went out as usual; but they never returned.

The whole country mourned, but the king was the one who sorrowed most. Messengers were sent out to search for them, both in his own and in foreign countries; proclamations were read out in all the churches, and the bells were rung all over the country. But they had disappeared and left no trace behind, so the people at last guessed that they had been spirited away into the mountains.

It did not take long before this was known far and wide, in town and country; yea, even in the very depth of the country and in foreign lands. And so the report reached the ears of a king in a far away country, who had twelve sons.

When they heard about the twelve princesses, they asked for leave to set out and find them. The king did not much like them to go; he was afraid he should never see them again. But they went on their knees before him, and prayed so long that the king at last gave his consent.

He fitted out a ship for them and gave them a knight called Redbeard as steersman, for he was a good seaman. They sailed about for a very long time and visited all the countries they came near, and asked and searched for the princesses, but they got no tidings whatever.

But a few more days and they would have been gone seven years. Then one day there blew such a gale and the weather was so bad that they believed they would never reach land any more. While the stormy weather lasted they were all obliged to work, so they got no rest. On the third day the wind went down and there came a calm.

Now they were all so tired after the hard work and rough weather that they fell asleep at once, but the youngest prince felt uneasy and could get no sleep.

While he paced backwards and forwards on deck the ship neared a small island, and on the shore was a little dog running about, barking and whining at the ship, just as if it wanted to be taken on board. The prince walked up and down on the deck, whistling and calling the dog, but the little creature only barked and whined the more.

The prince thought it was a great pity to leave it there to starve; he fancied it must have belonged to a ship which had been wrecked during the storm, but he did not think he could help it either, for he thought he would not be able to put the boat out without help, and all the crew slept so soundly he would not awake them for the sake of a dog.

But the weather was bright and calm, so he said to himself: "I had better go ashore and save the dog," and tried to lower the boat and found it was easily managed.

He rowed ashore and went up to the dog, but every time he tried to seize it the dog ran away from him, and this went on until before he knew a word about it he found himself in a large gilded castle. There the dog changed into a beautiful princess, and on the bench sat a man so big and ugly that the prince became quite terrified.

"You need not be frightened," said the man, but the prince became still more frightened when he heard his voice; "for I know very well what you want; you are the twelve princes who are looking for the twelve princesses that were lost. I know where they are; they are in my master's castle; there they sit on golden stools, each scratching a head, for he has twelve of them. Now you have been sailing about for seven years, but you will have to sail for seven more years before you find them. You might as well stay here," he said, "and wed my daughter; but first of all you must kill my master, for he is very hard on us. We are tired of him, and when he is dead I shall be king in his place. Try first if you can lift this sword," said the troll.

The prince took hold of an old rusty sword which hung on the wall, but he could scarcely stir it.

"Well then, you will have to take a drink from this bottle," said the troll.

When he had taken one sip he was just able to move the sword, and when he had taken another he could lift it, and when he had taken still another he could flourish the sword as easily as a rolling-pin.

"When you return on board," said the troll, "you must hide

the sword well in your berth, so that Knight Redbeard does not see it; he would not be able to use it, of course, but he hates you, and will try to take your life."

"Three days before the seven years are up," he said further, "all that has happened now will happen again; you will have bad and stormy weather, and when it is over you will all become sleepy; then you must take the sword and go ashore. You will then come to a castle where there are all sorts of sentinels—wolves, bears, and lions; but you must not be afraid of them, for they will all fall down before your feet. When you get into the castle you will see the troll-king sitting in a gorgeous chamber, magnificently dressed; he has twelve heads, and the princesses will be sitting on their golden stools, each of them scratching one of his heads. This kind of work, you know, they don't like, so you must make haste and cut off one head after the other; if the troll wakes up and sees you he will swallow you alive."

The prince went on board with the sword, and he remembered well what he had been told. All on board were still asleep, and he hid the sword in his berth, so that Knight Redbeard and the other could not see it. It then began to blow again, so the prince called the others and said he thought it would not do to sleep any longer since they had such a fair wind. Nobody guessed he had been away from the ship.

Now when the seven years all but three days had passed it happened just as the troll had said. There came bad and stormy weather which lasted for three days, and when it was over they all became sleepy after their hard work and lay down; but the youngest prince rowed ashore and the sentinels fell down before him, and so he came to the castle. When he entered the chamber the king-troll sat and slept just as the other troll had foretold, and the twelve princesses sat on their stools, each scratching one of his heads. The prince made signs to the princesses to move away, but they pointed at the troll and motioned to the prince to go.

He continued to make signs to them, and then they understood that he wanted to save them. They moved quietly away, one after the other, and immediately he cut off the heads of the troll-king, till the blood flowed like a great brook.

When the troll was killed, the prince rowed out to the ship again and hid the sword; he thought he had done his share, and as he could not get the body away by himself, he thought the others ought to help him a little. He therefore called them, and said it was a shame they should be lying asleep while he had been finding the princesses and had saved them from the troll-king.

The others laughed at him and said that, no doubt, he had been sleeping as well, if not better, than they, and had dreamt that he was such a clever fellow. If any one had saved the princesses, it was far more likely to be one of them.

But the youngest prince told them how it had all happened, and when they went ashore with him and saw the brook of blood, the castle, the troll, the twelve heads and the princesses, they saw he had told the truth; and so they helped him to throw the heads and the body into the sea.

They were now all quite happy, but none more so than the princesses, who after this, had no longer to sit all day and scratch the troll-king's heads. They took with them of all the gold and silver and valuable things which were there, as much as they could carry; and so they went on board, both the princes and the princesses.

When they had got a good way out to sea, the princesses said that in their joy they had forgotten their golden crowns; they lay in a chest, and they would so much like to take them with them. As none of the others offered to go for them, the youngest prince said:

"I have ventured as much before, so now I may as well fetch the crowns, if you will let down the sails and wait till I come back again."

Yes, that they would; but when he had got so far away that they could not see anything more of him, Knight Redbeard, who

THEN SUDDENLY SOMETHING CAME FLOPPING DOWN BY THE SIDE OF THE PRINCE'S BED

himself wanted to be foremost and have the youngest princess, said that it was of no use to lie and wait for him, for they must surely know he would never come back.

They knew, he said, that the king had given him, Knight Redbeard, power and authority to do just as he thought right; and they could say that he had saved the princesses, and if any one dared to say otherwise he should lose his life.

The princes therefore dared not do anything else but what Knight Redbeard told them, and so they set sail.

In the meantime, the youngest prince rowed ashore and went into the castle, found the chest, in which were the golden crowns, and tugged and dragged till he got it down to the boat; but when he came to the place where he expected to find the ship, it was gone. As he could not see it in any direction, he soon guessed what had happened, and there was therefore nothing else for him to do but to turn round and row to land again.

He was, of course, afraid to be alone the whole night in the castle, but there was no other shelter, so he took courage, locked all the doors and gates, and lay himself down in a room where there was a ready made bed. But he felt afraid, and became still more so, when, after he had been in bed awhile, the walls and roof began to creak and groan as if the whole castle was falling to pieces. Then, all of a sudden, something, which sounded like a load of hay, came flopping down by the side of his bed, and all became quiet again; but he heard a voice, which told him not to be afraid, and said:

> "I am bird Dauntless,
> All that I do is faultless;
> Be not afraid of me,
> For I will help you o'er the sea!"

"The first thing you must do in the morning, when you awake, is to go to the storehouse and fetch four barrels of rye for me; I must have that for breakfast, otherwise I can do nothing."

When the prince awoke in the morning, he saw an enormous bird with a feather at the back of its neck as thick as a small pine-tree. The prince went to the storehouse for the four barrels of rye, and when the bird had eaten it, he told the prince to hang the chest with the golden crowns on one side of his neck and to take as much gold and silver as would balance it and hang it on the other; then he asked the prince to get on his back and to hold on to the big feather on his neck. Off they started, whisking through the air at such a speed that it did not take long before they overtook the ship. The prince wanted to go on board and fetch the sword, because he was afraid somebody might see it, for the troll had told him it must not be seen by anybody; but bird Dauntless said they could not trouble about it now.

"Knight Redbeard is not likely to see it," said the bird; "but if you go on board he will try and take your life, as he wants to have the youngest princess; but you may rest easy about her for she puts a naked sword by her side every night, when she goes to bed."

After some time they reached the island, where the troll, whom the prince had first met, lived. There the prince was so well received that there was no end of festivities. The troll did not know how to treat him well enough, for he had killed his master and made him the king; he would gladly give him his daughter and half of his kingdom. But the prince had taken such a fancy to the youngest princess, that he could not rest and wanted every moment to set out again.

The troll asked him to take a rest and remain with him for a time, and told him the princesses had seven years to sail yet before they would get home. He also told him the same about the princess as bird Dauntless had done.

"You can rest easy about her; she places a naked sword by

WHEN HE SAW THE SHIP RIGHT IN FRONT OF HIM, HE LIFTED THE CLUB

her side in bed. If you don't believe me," said the troll, "you can go on board, when the ship passes here, and see for yourself, and fetch the sword. I must have that back in any case."

When the ship came sailing past the weather had been bad again, and when the prince went on board he found everybody asleep, the princesses each with a prince by her side; but the youngest lay alone with a naked sword beside her, and on the floor, in front of the bed, lay Knight Redbeard.

The prince found his sword and went ashore, without any one having discovered he had been on board; but still he was uneasy and wanted to be off, and when at last the seven years were nearly over, all but about three weeks, the troll said:

"Now you had better get ready to sail, since you will not remain with us. I will lend you my iron-boat, which goes of itself, if only you say 'Boat, sail on.' In the boat you will find an iron club, and that club you must lift, when you see the ship right in front of you; they will then have such a gale of wind, they will not think of looking for you. When you come alongside the ship, you must lift the club again, and they will then have such a hurricane, that they will have something else to do than be spying after you; when you have passed them, you must lift the club for the third time, taking care always to lay it down carefully, otherwise you will get such weather that both you and they will perish. When you reach land you need not trouble yourself about the boat; you need only give it a push, turn it round and say, 'Boat, go home the same way you came.'"

When the prince started he had much gold and silver and lots of fine things, and clothes and linen, which the troll-princess had made for him during his long stay there, so he was much richer than any of his brothers.

He had no sooner sat himself down in the boat and said: "Boat, sail on," than the boat set off, and when he saw the ship right in front of him he lifted the club; they then got such a gale of wind that they could not look his way. When he got alongside the ship he lifted the iron club again, and the weather became so bad and stormy that the white foam splashed up on all sides, and the waves washed over the deck, so that the people on board had something else to do than be spying after him; and when he was passing them he lifted the club for the third time, and then they had so much to look after that they had no time to find out who he could be. He reached land long before the ship, and when he had taken all his things out of the boat he shoved it out again, turned it round and said: "Boat, go home the same way you came!" and off the boat started.

He disguised himself as a sailor, and went to an old woman who lived in a wretched hut hard by; he told her he was a poor sailor and belonged to a big ship, which had been wrecked, and that he was the only one who had been saved. He then asked her if she would give him shelter for himself and the things he had saved.

"Bless me!" said the woman, "I don't think I can give any one lodgings; you see how it is here, I have nothing to lie upon myself, still less anything for others to lie upon."

The sailor said that did not matter; if he could only get a roof over his head he did not mind how he lay. She could not deny him that, if he would take things as he found them; so in the evening he brought his things to the hut.

No sooner were they in, than the woman, who was very fond of some new gossip to run about with, began to ask him who he was, where he came from, where he had been, where he was going, what he had with him, on what errand he was travelling, and if he had heard anything about the twelve princesses, who had disappeared so many years ago, and about many other things which she wanted to know and talk about.

But he said he felt poorly, and his head ached so much after the terrible weather, he could not give an account of anything; she would have to leave him in peace for some days, till he had taken a rest after all the work he had had to do; then she should know everything, and more besides.

The following day the old woman began again to question him, but the sailor had still such pains in his head he could not give an account of anything. But all at once he dropped a hint that perhaps he knew something about the princesses after all. The old woman ran at once with what she had heard to all the gossips in the neighbourhood, and one after the other came running and asking for news of the princesses, if he had seen them, if they were soon coming home, if they were on the way, and more of that kind. But he still complained that his head ached, so he could not answer them; but he could tell them this much, that if they had not been drowned in the storm they would arrive in a fortnight's time, or perhaps before; but he could not tell for certain if they were alive. He had seen them, but they might easily have gone to the bottom since then.

One of the old women ran to the palace with this news, and said there was a sailor in the hut of a certain old woman, that he had seen the princesses, and that they might be expected in a fortnight's time, or perhaps in a week.

When the king heard this he sent a messenger to fetch the sailor that he might come and tell the news himself.

"I am not in a fit state to go," said the sailor, "for I have no clothes good enough in which to appear before the King." But the King's messenger said he must come; the King would and must speak with him, no matter how he was dressed, for no one had as yet been able to tell the King anything about the princesses.

"Yes, I can," said the sailor. "But I cannot tell if they are still alive. When I saw them the weather was so bad that we were wrecked; but if they are still alive they will be here in a fortnight's time, or perhaps before."

When the King heard this he almost went out of his mind with joy; and as the time when the sailor had said they would return drew near, the King proceeded to the shore in great pomp to meet them.

There was great joy all over the country when the ship arrived with the princesses, the princes and Knight Redbeard; but no one was more glad than the old King, who now had got his daughters back again. The eleven elder princesses were very happy and merry, but the youngest, who was to have Knight Redbeard, was always weeping and sorrowful.

The King did not like this, and asked her why she was not merry and happy like her sisters; there was no reason why she should be so sad, now that she had escaped from the troll and was going to marry such a brave man as Knight Redbeard. But she dared not say anything, for Knight Redbeard had vowed he would take the life of any one who told how all had happened. One day when the princesses were busy making fine clothes for the weddings, a person dressed like a sailor, with a pack on his back, came into the palace, and asked if they would buy some pretty things from him for their wedding; he had many rare and costly articles both in gold and silver. Yes, they would look at his wares. Then they glanced at him and thought they recognised both him and many of the things he had.

"You, who have so many fine things," said the youngest princess, "must surely have many things which are still finer, and which would suit us still better."

"That may be," said the pedlar; but her sisters told her to be quiet, and reminded her what Knight Redbeard had threatened them with.

Some time afterwards the princesses were sitting one day by the window, when the youngest prince came by with the chest containing the golden crowns on his back.

When he came into the great hall of the palace he opened the chest for the princesses, and they all recognised their crowns. The youngest then said:

"I think it is only right that the one who saved us should have the reward he deserves. It is not Knight Redbeard, but he who has brought us our crowns—that has saved us." And then the prince threw off his sailor attire and stood before them more finely dressed than all the other princes, and the old King then ordered that Knight Redbeard should be put to death.

Now there was great joy in the palace. Each prince took his bride, and they kept such a wedding that it was heard of and talked about throughout twelve kingdoms.

THE TOWN MOUSE AND THE COUNTRY MOUSE

Once upon a time a town mouse met a country mouse on the outskirts of a wood. The country mouse was sitting under a hazel thicket plucking nuts.

"Busy harvesting, I see," said the town mouse. "Who would think of our meeting in this out-of-the-way part of the world?"

"Just so," said the country mouse.

"You are gathering nuts for your winter store?" said the town mouse.

"I am obliged to do so if we intend having anything to live upon during the winter," said the country mouse.

"The husk is big and the nut full this year, enough to satisfy any hungry body," said the town mouse.

"Yes, you are right there," said the country mouse; and then she related how well she lived and how comfortable she was at home.

The town mouse maintained that she was the better off, but the country mouse said that nowhere could one be so well off as in the woods and hills. The town mouse, however, declared she was best off; and as they could not agree on this point they promised to visit one another at Christmas, then they could see for themselves which was really the most comfortable.

The first visit was to be paid by the town mouse.

Now, although the country mouse had moved down from the mountains for the winter, the road was long and tiring and one had to travel up hill and down dale; the snow lay thick and deep, so the town mouse found it hard work to get on and she became both tired and hungry before she reached the end of her journey.

How nice it will be to get some food, she thought.

The country mouse had scraped together the best she had. There were nut kernels, polypoly and other sorts of roots, and many other good things which grow in woods and fields. She kept it all in a hole far under the ground, so the frost could not reach it, and close by was a running spring, open all the winter, so she could drink as much water as she liked. There was an abundance of all she had, and they ate both well and heartily; but the town mouse thought it was very poor fare indeed.

"One can, of course, keep body and soul together on this," said she; "but I don't think much of it. Now you must be good enough to visit me and taste what we have."

Yes, that she would, and before long she set out. The town mouse had gathered together all the scraps from the Christmas fare which the woman of the house had dropped on the floor during the holidays—bits of cheese, butter and tallow ends, cake-crumbs, pastry and many other good things. In the dish under the ale-tap she had drink enough; in fact, the place was full of all kinds of dainties.

They ate and fared well; the country mouse seemed never to have had enough; she had never tasted such delicacies. But then she became thirsty, for she found the food both strong and rich, and now she wanted something to drink.

"We haven't far to go for the beer we shall drink," said the town mouse, and jumped upon the edge of the dish and drank till she was no longer thirsty; she did not drink too much, for she knew the Christmas beer was strong. The country mouse, however, thought the beer a splendid drink; she had never tasted anything but water, so she took one sip after another, but as she could not stand strong drink she became tipsy before she left the dish.

The drink got into her head and down into her toes and she began running and jumping about from one beer barrel to the other, and to dance and tumble about on the shelves amongst the cups and mugs; she squeaked and screeched as if she were both drunk and mad. About her being drunk there was very little doubt.

"You must not carry on as if you had just come from the backwoods and make such a row and noise," said the town mouse: "the master of the house is a bailiff and he is very strict indeed," she added.

The country mouse said she didn't care either for bailiffs or beggars. But the cat sat at the top of the cellar steps, lying in wait, and heard all the chatter and noise. When the woman of the house went down to draw some beer and lifted the trap door the cat slipped by into the cellar and struck its claws into the country mouse. Then there was quite another sort of dance.

The town mouse slid back into her hole and sat in safety looking on, while the country mouse suddenly became sober when she felt the claws of the cat in her back.

"Oh, my dear bailiff, oh, dearest bailiff, be merciful and spare my life and I will tell you a fairy tale," she said.

"Well, go on," said the cat.

"Once upon a time there were two little mice," said the country mouse, squeaking slowly and pitifully, for she wanted to make the story last as long as she could.

"Then they were not lonely," said the cat dryly and curtly.

"And they had a steak which they were going to fry."

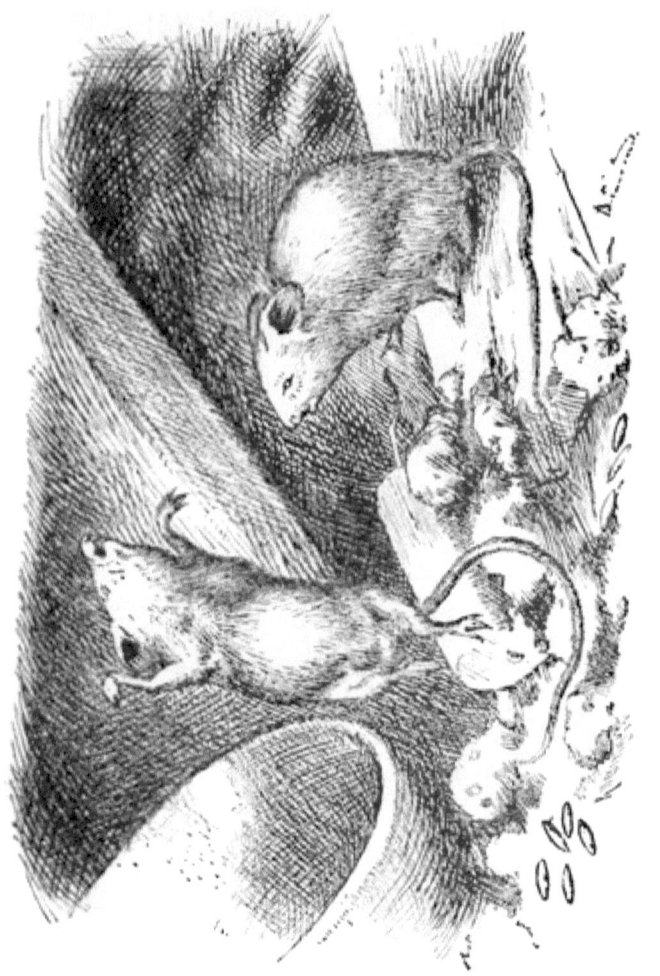

THE COUNTRY MOUSE BEGAN TO JUMP ABOUT AND DANCE, SQUEAKING AND SCREECHING AS IF SHE WERE DRUNK

THE TOWN MOUSE AND THE COUNTRY MOUSE 121

"Then they could not starve," said the cat.

"And they put it out on the roof to cool," said the country mouse.

"Then they did not burn themselves," said the cat.

"But there came a fox and a crow and ate it all up," said the country mouse.

"Then I'll eat you," said the cat. But just at that moment the woman shut the trap door with a slam, which so startled the cat that she let go her hold of the mouse. One bound, and the country mouse found herself in the hole with the town mouse.

From there a passage led out into the snow, and you may be sure the country mouse did not wait long before she set out homewards.

"And this is what you call living well and being best off," she said to the town mouse. "Heaven preserve me from having such a fine place and such a master! Why, I only just got away with my life!"

SORIA MARIA'S CASTLE

There was once upon a time a couple who had a son, and his name was Halvor. Since he was quite a small boy he never cared to do any work; he would only sit in the hearth and rake together the ashes. The parents had many times apprenticed him to learn some trade, but Halvor never stopped long anywhere; —when he had been at a place for some days he always ran off home again, sat himself down in the hearth, and began digging in the ashes.

But one day a skipper came to the house and asked Halvor if had a mind to go to sea with him and visit foreign countries. Yes, Halvor had a mind for that, and this time he was not long in getting ready.

How long they sailed I do not know, but after some time a storm overtook them and when it was over and the sea became calm they did not know where they were; they had drifted to a foreign coast which was quite unknown to them.

As there was no wind at all they had to remain there and Halvor asked the skipper for permission to go ashore and look about a bit, for he would rather do that than lie and sleep.

"Do you think you are fit to show yourself?" said the skipper. "Why you have no other clothes but the rags you have on your back." But Halvor would not give in, and at last he got permission; but he must come back on board when it began to blow.

He started off and found the country most beautiful; all around he saw large plains with cornfields and meadows, but he did not see any people. Soon it began to blow, but Halvor did not think he had seen enough yet, so he thought he would go on a little further and see if he could find any people.

In a while he came to a big road, which was so even one could roll an egg along it. Halvor followed the road, and towards evening he saw a great castle far away all lighted up.

As he had been walking all day almost without any food, he was very hungry; but the nearer he came to the castle the more afraid he felt.

In the castle the fires were still burning in the hearths. Halvor went into the kitchen, which was the most splendid he had ever seen; there were pots and pans both of gold and silver, but no people. When Halvor had stood there awhile and no one came, he went to a door and opened it and inside sat a princess at her spinning wheel.

"Oh dear! Oh dear!" she cried, "how dare any Christian person come here! You had better go away, if you don't want the troll to swallow you alive, for here lives a troll with three heads."

"It would be all one to me, even if he had four," said the lad. "I should much like to see him! I am not going away, for I have done nothing wrong; you must give me something to eat as I am terribly hungry."

When Halvor had finished his meal, the princess told him he had better try if he could swing the sword which hung on the wall. No, he could not even lift it.

"You had better take a drink from that bottle, which hangs by the side of it," said the princess, "for the troll does so, when he is going to use the sword."

Halvor took a drink, and immediately he was able to swing the sword as if it had been nothing. Now, thought he, the troll might come any time. All at once they heard the troll coming, and Halvor hid behind the door.

"Ugh! I smell Christian blood here," said the troll, putting one head in through the door.

"You'll soon find that is so," said Halvor, and cut off all his heads. The princess was so glad at being saved that she both sang and danced. Then she began to think about her sisters and said:

"I wish my sisters were saved also."

"Where are they?" asked Halvor; and so she told him one was shut up by a troll in a castle fifty miles away, and the other was shut up in a castle another fifty miles away.

"First you must help me to get this carcase away," said she. Halvor was so strong he swept everything before him, and cleared all away in no time; he then ate and enjoyed himself for the rest of the day.

Next morning he set out at daybreak, and so eager was he to

WHEN THE TROLL WITH THE THREE HEADS CAME INTO THE ROOM, HALVOR TOOK THE SWORD AND CUT OFF ALL THE HEADS

reach the castle, that he ran the whole day. When at last he saw it he became frightened again; it was more gorgeous even than the first one, but here also he could see no one. He went into the kitchen and straight on into the room without stopping.

"Oh, dear! how dare any Christian person come here!" cried the princess. "I don't know how long I have been here, but during all that time I have not seen a Christian. You had better go away, for here lives a troll who has six heads."

"No, I won't go," said Halvor, "even if he had twelve."

"He will swallow you alive," said the princess. But it was of no use, Halvor would not go; he was not afraid of the troll, but he wanted meat and drink, for he was hungry after the journey. He got as much as he wanted and then the princess again begged him to go.

"No," said Halvor, "I won't go, for I have done nothing wrong and I have nothing to be afraid of."

"That makes no difference," said the princess, "for he will take you, whether or no; but since you will not go, try if you can swing this sword, which the troll uses when he goes to war."

He could not swing the sword, so the princess told him to take a drink from the bottle which hung by the side. When he had done so, he found himself able to swing the sword. All of a sudden the troll came home; he was so fat and big he had to go sideways to get through the door. When he had got one of his heads inside he cried:

"Ugh! what a smell of Christian blood!" but at the same moment Halvor cut off one head and then all the others.

The princess was very glad, but she soon began to think of her sisters and wish that they also were saved. Halvor thought that could be done, and wanted to set off at once; but first he had to help the princess to get rid of the body of the troll, and next morning he set out.

It was a long way to the castle, and he walked and ran as fast as he could to get there in good time. Towards evening he came in sight of the castle, and found it even more splendid than the others. He was not the least afraid this time, but went straight through the kitchen and into the room. There sat the princess, who was so pretty that no words can tell. She said just the same as the other princesses, that no Christian person had been there since she came, and asked him to go away, or else the troll would swallow him alive. This troll had nine heads, she said.

"Well, even if he has twice nine and still another nine I shall not go," said Halvor, going up to the fire.

The princess entreated him to go, so that the troll should not eat him; but Halvor said: "Let him come when he likes;" then she gave him the sword and asked him to take a sip from the bottle, so that he could use the sword.

All of a sudden the troll came in with a great noise. He was still fatter and bigger than the other two, and he had also to go sideways to get through the door.

"Ugh! what a smell of Christian blood!" he said; but at the same moment Halvor cut off his first head and then all the others; but the last one was very tough and gave Halvor more work than anything he had yet had to do, although he felt so very strong.

All the princesses were now together at this castle, and they were happier than they had ever been in all their lives. They were very fond of Halvor and he of them. He could choose the one he liked best of them to wed, but the youngest was most fond of him of all three. He, however, went about looking so sad, and he was so sullen and quiet, that the princesses asked him what he was longing for and whether he did not like staying with them. Yes, that he liked well enough, for they had plenty to live on and he was very comfortable; but he longed so much for home, his parents were still alive, and he had a great mind to see them again. That could easily be arranged, they said:

"You can go there and back without any danger, if you follow our advice." Yes, he would do everything they told him. Then they dressed him up till he looked as fine as a prince, and they put a magic ring on his finger, so that he had only to wish himself anywhere and his wish would be fulfilled; but they said he must not lose the ring or mention their names, for then there would be an end to all their happiness and he would never see them any more.

"I wish I were home," said Halvor, and as he wished so it happened. He stood outside his parents' house in less than no time. It was just in the dusk of the evening, and when his parents saw what a fine and noble stranger was coming they lost their wits, and began to bow and curtsy. Halvor asked if he could stop there and get lodgings for the night.

No, that he couldn't. "Our place is not good enough," they said; "we have nothing here that would do for so grand a traveller." He had better go up to the farm, which was not far away; he could see the chimney-pots from where they stood, and there he would find plenty of everything. Halvor did not like that at all; he wanted to remain where he was, but the parents stuck to what they had said, that he should go up to the farm, for there he could get both meat and drink, while they had not even a chair to offer him.

"No," said Halvor, "I won't go there till the morning; let me remain here to-night; I can sit in the hearth." They could not refuse him that, so Halvor sat down in the hearth and began digging in the ashes, just as he had done when he was at home and idled away his time.

They spoke about a good many things, and told Halvor one thing and another till at last he asked them if they ever had had any children. Yes, they had a boy whose name was Halvor, but they did not know whereabouts he was wandering, or whether he was alive or dead.

"Could I be he?" said Halvor.

"No, not likely," said the woman; "Halvor was such a lazy, idle boy, he would never do anything, and he was so ragged his rags would hardly keep together; he could never become as grand as you."

In a little while the woman went over to the chimney to rake the fire, and just then the light from the ashes shone upon Halvor the same as when he used to sit at home raking in the ashes, and then the woman knew him again.

"Of course it is you, Halvor!" she said, and the old couple became so glad they did not know what to do. He had then to tell them all that had happened to him, and his mother was so proud of him that she wanted to take him up with her to the farm and show him off to the girls, who had always put on such airs. She went first and Halvor came after. When she got up there she told the people Halvor had come home again, and they should soon see what a fine fellow he was; he looked like a prince, she said.

"Oh, indeed!" said the girls, turning up their noses; "we expect he is the same ragged fellow as ever." Just at that moment Halvor came in, and so startled the girls, who were busy dressing themselves, that they took to their heels with nothing on but their petticoats.

When they came in again they were so shy they hardly dared to look at Halvor, to whom they had formerly always been so proud and short-spoken.

"Well, you have always thought yourselves so fine and handsome that there were none like you, but you should just see the eldest of the princesses I have saved," said Halvor; "by her side you would look like scullery-maids, and the second sister is still prettier; but the youngest, who is my sweetheart, is prettier than both the sun and the moon. I wish they were here, and then you would see," said Halvor.

He had no sooner spoken the words than the princesses stood there. This vexed him very much, for now he remembered his promise to them. Much rejoicing now began on the farm in honour of the princesses, but they did not care to remain there.

"We want to visit your parents," they said to Halvor, "and then we'll travel about and look around us." He said he would go with them, and soon they came to a large lake some distance from the farm. Close to the lake was a green hillside, where the princesses wanted to rest a while, for they thought it would be so nice to sit there and look out over the water.

THE PRINCESSES WANTED TO REST A WHILE, FOR THEY THOUGHT IT WOULD BE SO NICE TO SIT THERE AND LOOK OUT OVER THE WATER

They sat down, and after a while the youngest princess said to Halvor: "Won't you lie down and rest your head in my lap?" Yes, he would do so, and before long he fell asleep. Then she took the ring from his finger and put another in its place, and said to her sisters:

"Take hold of me as I take hold of you. I wish we were back in Soria Maria's castle."

When Halvor awoke he soon guessed he had lost the princesses and began to cry and lament, and was so disconsolate no one could get a word out of him. Though his parents begged and prayed him to stop with them he would not, but bid them farewell, and said he was not ever likely to see them again, for if he did not find the princesses life would not be worth living. He had three hundred dollars left which he put in his pocket, and then set out.

When he had got a bit on the way he met a man with a horse which he wanted to buy, so he began bargaining.

"Well, I have not exactly been thinking of selling it," said the man, "but if we can come to some agreement, well——" Halvor asked how much he wanted for it.

"I did not pay much for it, and it isn't worth much," said the man; "it is a good horse to ride on, but no good as a cart-horse. In any case he could manage to get along with your scrip-bag and you as well, if you will walk a bit now and then."

At last they agreed about the price, and Halvor put his bag on the horse, and sometimes walked and sometimes rode, till towards evening he came to a green field, and there stood a great tree, under which he sat down. He let the horse loose, and then opened his bag and had some food, but did not lie down to sleep.

At daylight he set out, for he had no peace of mind till he was on his way again; so he rode and walked by turns all day through a large forest with many beautiful green openings gleaming here and there among the trees. He did not know where he was, nor in which direction he was going; he only gave himself time to rest when he came to one of the green spots; he then foddered the horse and had some food himself.

On he walked and on he rode, and it seemed as if there never would be an end to the forest. But towards evening on the second day he saw a light shining between the trees. "I hope the folks are not gone to bed, so that I can warm myself and get something to eat," said Halvor to himself. When he came nearer he found only a poor little hut, and through the window he saw an old couple. They were very old and grey, and the woman had such a long nose that she could use it to rake the ashes together with when she sat by the fire.

"Good evening, good evening," said the woman. "But what business can you have here, I wonder? No Christian people have been this way for over a hundred years."

Halvor told her he was going to Soria Maria's castle, and asked her if she knew the way.

"No," said the old woman, "I don't know, but the moon will be out soon, and I'll ask her; she is sure to know, for she shines over every place."

As soon as the moon appeared bright and clear above the tree-tops, the woman went out.

"You moon! you moon!" she shouted, "can you tell me the way to Soria Maria's castle?"

"No," said the moon, "I cannot, for when I passed that way a cloud stood before me."

"Wait a while yet," said the woman to Halvor, "the west wind will be here directly; he is sure to know, for he whistles and blows in every corner. Dear, dear, you have a horse, I see," continued the old woman, as she came into the room. "Let the poor creature into the meadow; don't let it remain here at the door to starve. Will you exchange it with me for something?" said she. "We have a pair of old boots here, and when you have them on you can take twenty miles at every step. You can have them instead of the horse, and then you can get sooner to Soria Maria's castle."

Halvor agreed at once, and the woman took such a fancy to the horse she was ready to dance for joy, "For now I can ride to church like other people," she said.

Halvor became impatient to start, but the woman said there was no hurry.

THE OLD WOMAN WENT OUT TO ASK THE MOON THE WAY TO SORIA MARIA'S CASTLE

"Lie down on the bench and take a nap, for we have no bed," said she, "and I will look out for the west wind when he comes."

All of a sudden the west wind came rushing along, making the walls creak and groan. The woman ran out.

"You west wind! you west wind! can you tell me the way to Soria Maria's castle? There is somebody here who wants to go that way."

"Yes, I know it well," said the west wind. "I am just going there to dry clothes for a wedding which is to be. If he is quick on his legs he can come with me."

Halvor just then came out.

"You will have to make haste if you want company," said the west wind; and away they went far over hills and dales and seas, while Halvor had as much as he could do to keep up.

"I haven't time to go with you any further," said the west wind, "for I have to tear up a pine forest first before I go to the bleaching ground to dry the clothes; but if you keep along the ridge of the mountain you will come to some lasses who are washing clothes, and then you have not far to go to Soria Maria's castle."

Before long Halvor came to the lasses who were busy washing clothes. They asked if he had seen anything of the west wind.

"He was coming here to dry clothes for the wedding," said they.

"Yes," said Halvor, "he has only gone to tear up a pine forest; it will not be long before he is here." And then he asked them the way to Soria Maria's castle.

They put him in the way, and when he came to the castle he found quite a crowd of horses and people there. But Halvor was so ragged and dirty from having followed the west wind through bush and bog that he kept out of sight, and would not go to the castle till the last day, when they were going to have a grand dinner. And when the time came, as was the custom, for drinking the health of the bride, and the servant was filling every one's cup—that of the bride and bridegroom, the knights' and yeomen's—he came at length to Halvor.

He drank the toast, and let the ring which the princess had put on his finger at the lake fall into the cup. He then asked the servant to carry the cup to the bride, with his compliments.

The princess at once got up from the table.

"Who has most right to wed one of us," she said; "he who saved us or he who sits here as bridegroom?"

All thought there could be but one opinion about that; so when Halvor heard it, he was not long in getting off his rags and in dressing himself as a bridegroom.

"Yes, he is the right one!" cried the youngest princess when she saw him; and so she threw the other one over, and was married to Halvor.

WELL DONE, ILL PAID

Once upon a time there was a man who was going to the forest for firewood. On his way he met a bear.

"Give me your horse, or I will kill all your sheep next summer!" said the bear.

"Oh dear! oh dear!" said the man, "there is not a chip of wood in the house. You must let me drive home a cartload of wood, or we shall be frozen to death; but I will come back with the horse to-morrow for you."

Well, that would do; but it was understood that if he did not return he would lose all his sheep during the summer. The man loaded his sledge with wood, and drove homewards; but he was not very pleased with the arrangement he had made, you can imagine. On the way he met a fox.

"Why do you look so sad?" asked the fox.

"Oh, I met a bear up yonder," said the man, "and I had to promise that at this time to-morrow he should have my horse. If he does not get it, he said he would tear all my sheep to pieces next summer."

"Oh, nothing worse than that?" said the fox. "If you will give me your fattest ram I will soon get you out of your difficulty."

The man promised this, and said he would be sure to keep his word.

"When you come to the bear to-morrow with the horse," said the fox, "I will be up in the mountain, and will shout out to you. When the bear asks who it is, you must say it is Peter, the huntsman, who is the finest shot in the world. Afterwards you must use your own wits."

The next day the man set out, and when he met the bear some one up in the mountain began shouting.

"Whst! what's that?" said the bear.

"Oh, that's Peter, the huntsman. He is the finest shot in the world," said the man. "I know him by his voice."

"Have you seen any bear about here, Erik?" came from the wood.

"Say no!" said the bear.

"No, I have not seen any bear," said Erik.

"What's that standing by your sledge then?" came from the wood.

"Say it is the root of an old tree," whispered the bear.

"Oh, it's only the root of an old tree," said Erik.

"Such roots we generally load our sledges with," came from the wood; "if you are not able to do so, I will come and help you."

"Say you can do it yourself, and put me on the sledge."

"No, thanks, I can manage by myself," said the man, and rolled the bear on to the sledge.

"Such roots we generally tie down," came from the wood; "do you want any help?"

"Say you can do it yourself, and tie me down," said the bear.

"No, thanks, I can do it," said Erik, and began tying down the bear with all the ropes he had, till the bear could not move a paw.

"Such roots we generally strike an axe into, when we have tied it down," come from the wood, "for then one can steer the sledge better down the big hills."

"Pretend to strike the axe into me," whispered the bear.

But the man took the axe and split the skull of the bear, who was killed on the spot. So Erik and the fox became good friends and got on well together, but when they came to the farm, the fox said:

"I should like to go in with you, but I don't like your dogs. I will wait here till you come with the ram. But remember to pick me out one that is very fat."

Yes, the man would do so, and thanked the fox besides for his help. When he had put the horse into the stable he went across to the sheep-pen.

"Where are you going?" asked his wife.

"Oh, I am only going over to the sheep-pen to fetch a fat ram for that good fox who saved our horse," said the man, "as I have promised him one."

"Why on earth give that thief of a fox any ram?" said the woman. "We have got the horse quite safe and the bear besides, and the fox has stolen more geese from us than the ram is worth; or, if he hasn't already taken them, he is sure to do so sometime. No, take the most savage pair of those dogs of yours and let loose on him, then perhaps we'll get rid of that thieving old rascal," said the woman.

The man thought this was sensible advice and took two of his savage red dogs, put them in a bag and set out with them.

"Have you got the ram?" said the fox.

"Yes, come and fetch it," said the man, undoing the string round the bag and setting the dogs at the fox.

"Ugh!" said the fox bounding away, "the old saying, 'Well done, ill paid' is only too true; and now I find it is also true that one's relations are one's worst enemies," said he, as he saw the red dogs at his heels.

ASHIEPATTLE AND HIS GOODLY CREW

Once upon a time there was a king, and this king had heard about a ship which went just as fast by land as by water; and as he wished to have one like it, he promised any one who could build one for him, his daughter and half the kingdom. And this was given out at every church all over the country. There were many who tried, as you can imagine; for they thought it would be a nice thing to have half the kingdom, and the princess wouldn't be a bad thing into the bargain. But they all fared badly.

Now there were three brothers, who lived far away on the borders of a forest; the eldest was called Peter, the second Paul, and the youngest Espen Ashiepattle, because he always sat in the hearth, raking and digging in the ashes.

Ashiepattle and his Goodly Crew

It so happened that Ashiepattle was at church on the Sunday when the proclamation about the ship, which the king wanted, was read. When he came home and told his family, Peter the eldest asked his mother to get some food ready for him, for now he was going away to try if he could build the ship and win the princess and half the kingdom. When the bag was ready he set out. On the way he met an old man who was very crooked and decrepit.

"Where are you going?" said the man.

"I'm going into the forest to make a trough for my father. He doesn't like to eat at table in our company," said Peter.

"Trough it shall be!" said the man. "What have you got in that bag of yours?" he added.

"Dung," said Peter.

"Dung it shall be," said the man. Peter then went into the forest and began to cut and chop away at the trees and work away as hard as he could, but in spite of all his cutting and chopping he could only turn out troughs. Towards dinner time he wanted something to eat and opened his bag. But there was not a crumb of food in it. As he had nothing to live upon and as he did not turn out anything but troughs, he became tired of the work, took his axe and bag on his shoulder and went home to his mother.

Paul then wanted to set out to try his luck at building the ship and winning the princess and half the kingdom. He asked his mother for provisions, and when the bag was ready he threw it over his shoulder and went on his way to the forest. On the road he met the old man, who was very crooked and decrepit.

"Where are you going?" said the man.

"Oh, I am going into the forest to make a trough for our sucking pig," said Paul.

"Pig-trough it shall be," said the man. "What have you got in that bag of yours?" added the man.

"Dung," said Paul.

"Dung it shall be," said the man.

Paul then began felling trees and working away as hard as he could, but no matter how he cut and how he worked he could only turn out pig-troughs. He did not give in, however, but worked away till far into the afternoon before he thought of taking any food; then all at once he became hungry and opened his bag, but not a crumb could he find. Paul became so angry he turned the bag inside out and struck it against the stump of a tree; then he took his axe, went out of the forest and set off homewards.

As soon as Paul returned, Ashiepattle wanted to set out and asked his mother for a bag of food.

"Perhaps I can manage to build the ship and win the princess and half the kingdom," said he.

"Well, I never heard the like," said his mother. "Are you likely to win the princess, you, who never do anything but root and dig in the ashes? No, you shan't have any bag with food!"

Ashiepattle did not give in, however, but he prayed and begged till he got leave to go. He did not get any food, not he; but he stole a couple of oatmeal cakes and some flat beer and set out.

When he had walked awhile he met the same old man, who was so crooked and tattered and decrepit.

"Where are you going?" said the man.

"Oh, I was going into the forest to try if it were possible to build a ship which can go as fast by land as by water," said Ashiepattle, "for the king has given out that any one who can build such a ship shall have the princess and half the kingdom."

"What have you got in that bag of yours?" said the man.

"Not much worth talking about; there ought to be a little food in it," answered Ashiepattle.

"If you'll give me a little of it I'll help you," said the man.

"With all my heart," said Ashiepattle, "but there is nothing but some oatmeal cakes and a drop of flat beer."

It didn't matter what it was, the man said; if he only got some of it he would be sure to help Ashiepattle.

When they came up to an old oak in the wood the man said to the lad, "Now you must cut off a chip and then put it back

THE SHIP WHICH WENT JUST AS FAST BY LAND AS BY WATER

again in exactly the same place, and when you have done that you can lie down and go to sleep." Ashiepattle did as he was told and then lay down to sleep, and in his sleep he thought he heard somebody cutting and hammering and sawing and carpentering, but he could not wake up till the man called him; then the ship stood quite finished by the side of the oak.

"Now you must go on board and every one you meet you must take with you," said the man. Espen Ashiepattle thanked him for the ship, said he would do so, and then sailed away.

When he had sailed some distance, he came to a long, thin tramp, who was lying near some rocks, eating stones.

"What sort of a fellow are you, that you lie there eating stones?" asked Ashiepattle. The tramp said he was so fond of meat he could never get enough, therefore he was obliged to eat stones. And then he asked if he might go with him in the ship.

"If you want to go with us, you must make haste and get on board," said Ashiepattle.

Yes, that he would, but he must take with him some large stones for food.

When they had sailed some distance, they met one who was lying on the side of a sunny hill, sucking at a bung.

"Who are you," said Ashiepattle, "and what is the good of lying there sucking that bung?"

"Oh, when one hasn't got the barrel, one must be satisfied with the bung," said the man. "I'm always so thirsty, I can never get enough beer and wine." And then he asked for leave to go with him in the ship.

"If you want to go with me you must make haste and get on board," said Ashiepattle.

Yes, that he would. And so he went on board and took the bung with him to allay his thirst.

When they had sailed awhile again, they met one who was lying with his ear to the ground, listening.

"Who are you, and what is the good of lying there on the ground listening?" said Ashiepattle.

"I'm listening to the grass, for I have such good ears that I can hear the grass growing," said the man. And then he asked for leave to go with him in the ship. Ashiepattle could not say nay to that, so he said:

"If you want to go with me, you must make haste and get on board."

Yes, that the man would. And he also went on board.

When they had sailed some distance, they came to one who was standing taking aim with a gun.

"Who are you, and what is the good of standing there aiming like that?" asked Ashiepattle.

So the man said:

"I have such good eyes that I can hit anything, right to the end of the world." And then he asked for leave to go with him in the ship.

"If you want to go with me, you must make haste and get on board," said Ashiepattle.

Yes, that he would. And he went on board.

When they had sailed some distance again, they came to one who was hopping and limping about on one leg, and on the other he had seven ton weights.

"Who are you," said Ashiepattle, "and what is the good of hopping and limping about on one leg with seven ton weights on the other?"

"I am so light," said the man, "that if I walked on both my legs I should get to the end of the world in less than five minutes." And then he asked for leave to go with him in the ship.

"If you want to go with us, you must make haste and get on board," said Ashiepattle.

Yes, that he would. And so he joined Ashiepattle and his crew on the ship.

When they had sailed on some distance, they met one who was standing holding his hand to his mouth.

"Who are you?" said Ashiepattle, "and what is the good of standing there, holding your mouth like that?"

TO THE END OF THE WORLD IN LESS THAN FIVE MINUTES

"Oh, I have seven summers and fifteen winters in my body," said the man; "so I think I ought to keep my mouth shut, for if they get out all at the same time they would finish off the world altogether." And then he asked for leave to go with him in the ship.

"If you want to go with us, you must make haste and get on board," said Ashiepattle.

Yes, that he would, and then he joined the others on the ship.

When they had sailed a long time, they came to the king's palace.

Ashiepattle went straight in to the king and said the ship stood ready in the courtyard outside; and now he wanted the princess, as the king had promised.

The king did not like this very much, for Ashiepattle did not cut a very fine figure; he was black and sooty, and the king did not care to give his daughter to such a tramp, so he told Ashiepattle that he would have to wait a little.

"But you can have her all the same, if by this time to-morrow you can empty my storehouse of three hundred barrels of meat," said the king.

"I suppose I must try," said Ashiepattle; "but perhaps you don't mind my taking one of my crew with me?"

"Yes, you can do that, and take all six if you like," said the king, for he was quite sure that even if Ashiepattle took six hundred with him, it would be impossible. So Ashiepattle took with him the one who ate stones and always hungered after meat.

When they came next morning and opened the storehouse, they found he had eaten all the meat, except six small legs of mutton, one for each of his companions. Ashiepattle then went to the king and said the storehouse was empty, and he supposed he could now have the princess.

The king went into the storehouse, and, sure enough, it was quite empty; but Ashiepattle was still black and sooty and the king thought it was really too bad that such a tramp should have his daughter. So he said he had a cellar full of beer and old wine, three hundred barrels of each kind, which he would have him drink first.

"I don't mind your having my daughter if you can drink them up by this time to-morrow," said the king.

"I suppose I must try," said Ashiepattle, "but perhaps you don't mind my taking one of my crew with me?"

"Yes, you may do that," said the king, for he was quite sure there was too much beer and wine even for all seven of them. Ashiepattle took with him the one who was always sucking the bung, and was always thirsty; and the king then shut them down in the cellar.

There the thirsty one drank barrel after barrel, as long as there was any left, but in the last barrel he left a couple of pints to each of his companions.

In the morning the cellar was opened and Ashiepattle went at once to the king and said he had finished the beer and wine, and now he supposed he could have the princess as the king had promised.

"Well, I must first go down to the cellar and see," said the king, for he could not believe it; but when he got there he found nothing but empty barrels.

But Ashiepattle was both black and sooty, and the king thought it wouldn't do for him to have such a son-in-law. So he said, that if Ashiepattle could get water from the end of the world in ten minutes for the princess's tea, he could have both her and half the kingdom; for he thought that task would be quite impossible.

"I suppose I must try," said Ashiepattle, and sent for the one of his crew who limped about on one leg, and had seven ton weights on the other, and told him he must take off the weights and use his legs as quickly as he could, for he must have water from the end of the world for the princess's tea in ten minutes.

So he took off the weights, got a bucket and set off, and the next moment he was out of sight. But they waited and waited and still he did not return. At last it wanted but three minutes to the time, and the king became as pleased as if he had won a big wager. Then Ashiepattle called the one who could hear the grass grow and told him to listen and find out what had become of their companion.

"He has fallen asleep at the well," said he who could hear the grass grow; "I can hear him snoring, and a troll is scratching his head." Ashiepattle then called the one who could shoot to the end of the world, and told him to send a bullet into the troll; he did so and hit the troll right in the eye. The troll gave such a yell that he woke the man who had come to fetch the water for the tea, and when he returned to the palace there was still one minute left out of the ten.

Ashiepattle went straight to the king and said: "Here is the water"; and now he supposed he could have the princess, for surely the king would not make any more fuss about it now. But the king thought that Ashiepattle was just as black and sooty as ever, and did not like to have him for a son-in-law; so he said he had three hundred fathoms of wood with which he was going to dry corn in the bakehouse, and he wouldn't mind Ashiepattle having his daughter if he would first sit in the bakehouse and burn all the wood; he should then have the princess, and that without fail. "I suppose I must try," said Ashiepattle; "but perhaps you don't mind my taking one of my crew with me?"

"Oh no, you can take all six," said the king, for he thought it would be warm enough for all of them.

Ashiepattle took with him the one who had fifteen winters and seven summers in his body, and in the evening he went across to the bakehouse; but the king had piled up so much wood on the fire that you might almost have melted iron in the room. They could not get out of it, for no sooner were they inside than the king fastened the bolt and put a couple of padlocks on the door besides. Ashiepattle then said to his companion:

"You had better let out six or seven winters, so that we may get something like summer weather here."

They were then just able to exist, but during the night it got cold again and Ashiepattle then told the man to let out a couple of summers, and so they slept far into the next day. But when they heard the king outside, Ashiepattle said:

"You must let out a couple more winters, but you must manage it so that the last winter you let out strikes the king right in the face."

He did so, and when the king opened the door, expecting to find Ashiepattle and his companion burnt to cinders, he saw them huddling together and shivering with cold till their teeth chattered. The same instant Ashiepattle's companion with the fifteen winters in his body let loose the last one right in the king's face, which swelled up into a big chilblain.

"Can I have the princess now?" asked Ashiepattle.

"Yes, take her and keep her and the kingdom into the bargain," said the king, who dared not refuse any longer. And so the wedding took place and they feasted and made merry and fired off guns and powder.

While the people were running about searching for wadding for their guns, they took me instead, gave me some porridge in a bottle and some milk in a basket, and fired me right across here, so that I could tell you how it all happened.

GUDBRAND ON THE HILL-SIDE

THERE was once upon a time a man whose name was Gudbrand. He had a farm which lay far away up on the side of a hill, and therefore they called him Gudbrand on the hill-side.

He and his wife lived so happily together, and agreed so well, that whatever the man did the wife thought it so well done that no one could do it better. No matter what he did, she thought it was always the right thing.

They lived on their own farm, and had a hundred dollars at the bottom of their chest and two cows in their cowshed. One day the woman said to Gudbrand:

"I think we ought to go to town with one of the cows and sell it, so that we may have some ready money by us. We are pretty well off, and ought to have a few shillings in our pocket like other people; the hundred dollars in the chest we mustn't touch, but I can't see what we want with more than one cow, and it will be much better for us, as I shall have only one to look after instead of the two I have now to mind and feed."

Yes, Gudbrand thought, that was well and sensibly spoken. He took the cow at once and went to town to sell it; but when he got there no one would buy the cow.

"Ah, well!" thought Gudbrand, "I may as well take the cow home again. I know I have both stall and food for it, and the way home is no longer than it was here." So he strolled homewards again with the cow.

When he had got a bit on the way he met a man who had a horse to sell, and Gudbrand thought it was better to have a horse than a cow, and so he changed the cow for the horse.

When he had gone a bit further he met a man who was driving a fat pig before him, and then he thought it would be better to have a fat pig than a horse, and so he changed with the man.

He now went a bit further, and then he met a man with a goat, and so he thought it was surely better to have a goat than a pig, and changed with the man who had the goat.

Then he went a long way, till he met a man who had a sheep; he changed with him, for he thought it was always better to have a sheep than a goat.

When he had got a bit further he met a man with a goose, and so he changed the sheep for the goose. And when he had gone a long, long way he met a man with a cock; he changed the goose with him, for he thought this wise: "It is surely better to have a cock than a goose."

He walked on till late in the day, when he began to feel hungry. So he sold the cock for sixpence and bought some food for himself; "for it is always better to keep body and soul together than to have a cock," thought Gudbrand.

He then set off again homewards till he came to his neighbour's farm and there he went in.

"How did you get on in town?" asked the people.

"Oh, only so-so," said the man, "I can't boast of my luck, nor can I grumble at it either." And then he told them how it had gone with him from first to last.

"Well, you'll have a fine reception when you get home to your wife," said the man. "Heaven help you! I should not like to be in your place."

"I think I might have fared much worse," said Gudbrand; "but whether I have fared well or ill, I have such a kind wife that she never says anything, no matter what I do."

"Aye, so you say; but you won't get me to believe it," said the neighbour.

"Shall we have a wager on it?" said Gudbrand. "I have a hundred dollars in my chest at home; will you lay the same?"

So they made the wager and Gudbrand remained there till the evening, when it began to get dark, and then they went together to the farm.

The neighbour was to remain outside the door and listen, while Gudbrand went in to his wife.

"Good evening!" said Gudbrand when he came in.

"Good evening!" said the wife. "Heaven be praised you are back again."

"Yes, here I am!" said the man. And then the wife asked him how he had got on in town.

"Oh, so-so," answered Gudbrand; "not much to brag of. When I came to town no one would buy the cow, so I changed it for a horse."

"Oh, I'm so glad of that," said the woman; "we are pretty well off and we ought to drive to church like other people, and when we can afford to keep a horse I don't see why we should not have one. Run out, children, and put the horse in the stable."

"Well, I haven't got the horse after all," said Gudbrand; "for when I had got a bit on the way I changed it for a pig."

"Dear me!" cried the woman, "that's the very thing I should have done myself. I'm so glad of that, for now we can have some bacon in the house and something to offer people when they come to see us. What do we want with a horse? People would only say we had become so grand that we could no longer walk to church. Run out, children, and let the pig in."

"But I haven't got the pig either," said Gudbrand, "for when I had got a bit further on the road I changed it into a milch goat."

"Dear! dear! how well you manage everything!" cried the wife. "When I really come to think of it, what do I want with the pig? People would only say, 'over yonder they eat up everything they have.' No, now I have a goat I can have both milk and cheese and keep the goat into the bargain. Let in the goat, children."

"But I haven't got the goat either," said Gudbrand; "when I got a bit on the way I changed the goat and got a fine sheep for it."

"Well!" shouted the woman, "you do everything just as I should wish it—just as if I had been there myself. What do we want with a goat? I should have to climb up hill and down dale to get it home at night. No, when I have a sheep I can have wool and clothes in the house, and food as well. Run out, children, and let in the sheep."

"But I haven't got the sheep any longer," said Gudbrand, "for when I had got a bit on the way I changed it for a goose."

"Well, thank you for that!" said the woman; "and many thanks too! What do I want with a sheep? I have neither wheel nor spindle, and I do not care either to toil and drudge making clothes; we can buy clothes now as before. Now I can have goose-fat, which I have so long been wishing for, and some feathers to stuff that little pillow of mine. Run, children, and let in the goose."

"Well, I haven't got the goose either," said Gudbrand. "When I had got a bit further on the way I changed it for a cock."

"HAVE I WON THE HUNDRED DOLLARS NOW?" ASKED GUDBRAND

"Well, I don't know how you can think of it all!" cried the woman. "It's just as if I had done it all myself.—A cock! Why, it's just the same as if you'd bought an eight-day clock, for every morning the cock will crow at four, so we can be up in good time. What do we want with a goose? I can't make goose-fat and I can easily fill my pillow with some soft grass. Run, children, and let in the cock."

"But I haven't got a cock either," said Gudbrand, "for when I had got a bit further I became so terribly hungry I had to sell the cock for sixpence and get some food to keep body and soul together."

"Heaven be praised you did that!" cried the woman. "Whatever you do, you always do the very thing I could have wished. Besides, what did we want with the cock? We are our own masters and can lie as long as we like in the mornings. Heaven be praised! As long as I have got you back again, who manage everything so well, I shall neither want cock, nor goose, nor pig, nor cows."

Gudbrand then opened the door. "Have I won the hundred dollars now?" he asked. And the neighbour was obliged to confess that he had.

THE TWELVE WILD DUCKS

THERE was once upon a time a queen who was out driving one winter after a fresh fall of snow. When she had been driving some time her nose began to bleed and she got out of the sledge. While she was standing by the fence looking at the red blood on the white snow she began thinking that she had twelve sons, but no daughters; so she said to herself: "If I had a daughter as white as snow and as red as blood I should not care what became of my sons." The words were scarcely out of her mouth when a witch came up to her.

"You shall have a daughter," said she, "and she shall be as white as snow and as red as blood. Your sons shall then be mine, but you can keep them with you until the child is christened."

When the time came the queen had a daughter, and she was as white as snow and as red as blood, just as the witch had promised, and they therefore called her Snow-white-and-rosy-red.

There was great joy in the king's palace and the queen was happy beyond description, but when she remembered what she had promised the witch she ordered a silversmith to make twelve silver spoons, one for each prince; she also let him make one more, which she gave to Snow-white-and-rosy-red. As soon as the princess was christened the princes were changed into twelve wild ducks which flew away and no more was seen of them. Away they were and away they remained.

The princess grew up tall and fair, but she was often strange and sad and no one knew what ailed her. One evening the queen also felt very sad, for she was no doubt troubled whenever she thought of her sons, so she said to Snow-white-and-rosy-red:

"Why are you so sad, my daughter? If there is anything you want you shall have it."

"Oh, I think it is so lonely here," said the princess. "Every one has brothers and sisters, but I am all alone and have none. It is that which makes me so sad."

"You have had some brothers, my daughter," said the queen. "I had twelve sons, who were your brothers, but I gave them all away to get you," she said, and then she told her the whole story.

When the princess heard this she had no peace. She must and would set out to find her brothers. The queen cried and wept, but it was of no avail, for the princess thought she was the cause of it all, and at last she left the palace and set out on her search.

She walked and walked so far out in the wide world that no one would believe such a frail maiden could walk so far.

One day when she had been walking a long, long while in a great, big forest she became tired and sat down on a tussock and there she fell asleep. She dreamt she went further into the forest and came to a small log hut and there she found her brothers. Just then she awoke and straight in front of her she saw a path in the greensward leading further into the forest. She followed this, and after a long while she came to just such a little log hut as she had dreamt about.

When she got inside she found no one there, but there were twelve beds, and twelve stools, and twelve spoons, and twelve of everything that was in the place. When she saw this she became so glad, she had not felt so glad for many years; for she knew at once that her brothers lived there and that it was they who owned the beds, the stools, and the spoons. She began to make the fire and the beds, and to sweep out the room, and cook the food, and to tidy everything as best she could.

After she had done the cooking she had some food herself, but she forgot to take her spoon from the table. She then crept under the youngest brother's bed and lay down there.

No sooner had she done this than she heard a whizzing sound in the air and all the twelve wild ducks came flying in, but as soon as they had passed the threshold they at once became princes again.

"How nice and warm it is here!" they said. "Heaven bless the one who has made our fire and cooked such good food for us." And so they each took their silver spoon and sat down to eat. But when each had taken his own there was still one left lying on the table and it was so like the others that they could not tell the difference. They then looked at one another in great wonder.

"It is our sister's spoon," they said, "and if the spoon is here, she cannot be far away herself."

"If it is our sister's spoon and we find her here, she ought to be killed; for she is the cause of all our sufferings," said the eldest of the princes, and this the sister heard as she lay under the bed.

"No," said the youngest, "it would be a shame to kill her for it; she cannot be blamed that we suffer. If any one is the cause of it, it is our own mother." They then began to search for her, high and low, and at last they searched under all the beds, and when they came to that of the youngest prince they found her and dragged her out.

The eldest prince again said she ought to be killed, but she cried and prayed so pitifully for herself:

"Oh, pray do not kill me," she said; "I have been wandering about for many years searching for you. If I could save you, I would willingly give my life!"

"If you'll set us free, you shall live; for if you will, you can," said they.

"Only tell me how it can be done, and I'll do it, whatever it may be," said the princess.

"You must gather cotton-grass," said the princes, "and this you must card and spin and weave; when you have done that, you must cut out and make twelve caps, twelve shirts, and twelve handkerchiefs with the cloth, one for each of us; and while you do that, you must neither speak, nor laugh, nor weep. If you can do all that, we are saved."

"But where shall I get the cotton-grass for so many handkerchiefs and caps and shirts?" said their sister.

"That we will show you," said the princes; and so they took her with them to a great, big moor, which was covered with cotton-grass, waving in the wind and glistening in the sun, so that it shone like snow a long way off.

The princess had never seen so much before. She set to work at once to pluck and gather the best, as fast as she could, and in the evening when she came home, she began carding and spinning yarn from the down of the cotton-grass.

Thus all went well for a long time. She gathered the grass and carded it, and in the meantime she looked after the house for her brothers. She cooked their food and made their beds for them. In the evening they came flying home as wild ducks, and at night they were princes; but in the morning they flew away again, and were wild ducks the whole of the day.

But then it happened while she was on the moor gathering cotton-grass one day—and if I don't make a mistake it was the last time she had to go there—that a young king, who governed that country, was out shooting and came riding across the moor. When he saw her, he stopped and wondered who the beautiful maiden could be who was wandering about gathering cotton-grass. He asked her, but got no answer, and he then asked her again and wondered still more who she could be.

He took such a fancy to her that he wanted to take her home with him to the palace and marry her. He told his servants to take her and place her next him on his horse.

The princess wrung her hands, and made signs to them, pointing to the bags in which she had all her work; and when the king understood that she wanted these with her, he told his servants to take the bags with them.

When the princess saw this, she became contented, for the king was both good and handsome, and he was as kind and gentle to her as a child to a doll.

When they came home to the palace, and the old queen, who was the king's stepmother, saw Snow-white-and-rosy-red, she became so angry and jealous because she was so beautiful, that she said to the king:

"Can't you see that this woman whom you have taken with you and want to marry is a witch; she neither speaks, nor laughs, nor weeps."

The king did not listen to what she said, but married Snow-white-and-rosy-red, and they lived in great joy and splendour; but for all that she did not forget she had to make the shirts and caps for her brothers.

Before the year was over the young queen had a little prince, and this made the old queen still more angry and jealous. In the

SHE WAS ON THE MOOR GATHERING COTTON-GRASS

night she stole into the room where the queen slept, took the child and threw it into the snake-pit; she then cut the young queen's finger and smeared the blood on her mouth and went to the king.

"Come and see," she said, "whom you have taken for your queen, she has eaten her own child!"

The king then became so distressed that he nearly wept, and said:

"I suppose it must be true, since I have seen it with my own eyes, but surely she will not do it again. This time I will spare her life."

Before the next year was out she had another son, and the same thing happened again. The king's stepmother became still more jealous and angry; she stole into the queen's bedroom while she slept, took her child and threw it into the snake pit, cut the queen's finger, smeared the blood round her mouth, and then told the king that she had eaten this child also.

You can hardly imagine how distressed the king became, and then he said:

"I suppose it must be true, since I have seen it with my own eyes; but surely she will not do it again, and I'll spare her life this time also."

Before the following year was over the queen had a daughter, whom the old queen also took and threw into the snake-pit. While the young queen slept she cut her finger and smeared the blood around her mouth, and then went to the king and said:

"Now come and see if it isn't true what I have said, that she is a witch; for now she has eaten her third child also."

The king's sorrow was so great there was no end to it. He could not spare her life any longer, but was obliged to give orders that she should be burnt alive.

When the pile was lighted, and she was about to be placed on it, she made signs to the people to take twelve boards and place them round the pile. On these she laid all the handkerchiefs, and caps, and shirts for her brothers; but the left sleeve was wanting in the youngest brother's shirt, for she had not been able to get it ready. No sooner was this done, than they heard a whiz and a whirr in the air, and the twelve wild ducks came flying across from the forest. Each one took his clothes in his bill and flew off.

"You can see now," said the wicked queen to the king, "she is really a witch; make haste and burn her before the pile is burnt out."

"Oh," said the king, "we have plenty of wood; the forest is close at hand. I want to wait a bit, for I should like to see what the end of all this will be."

Just then the twelve princes came riding along the road, all as handsome and well-made as one could wish to see; but the youngest prince had a duck's wing instead of a left arm.

"What does all this mean?" asked the princes.

"My queen is to be burnt because she is a witch, and has eaten her own children;" answered the king.

"She has not eaten her children," said the prince. "Speak sister! Now that you have saved us, save yourself!"

Then Snow-white-and-rosy-red spoke and told them how all had happened, that every time a child was born the old queen, the king's stepmother, had stolen into her room in the night, taken the child from her, and cut her finger, and smeared the blood around her mouth.

The princes then took the king and led him to the snake-pit. There lay the three children playing with snakes and toads, and finer children you could not see anywhere. The king took them with him, and carried them to his stepmother, and asked her what punishment she thought ought to be given to any one who could be wicked enough to betray an innocent queen and three innocent children.

"He ought to be tied between twelve wild horses, and torn to pieces," said the old queen.

"You have pronounced your own doom, and now you will

THERE LAY THE THREE CHILDREN PLAYING WITH SNAKES AND TOADS

have to submit to it," said the king. And so the wicked old queen was tied between twelve wild horses and torn to pieces.

But Snow-white-and-rosy-red took the king and her children and the twelve princes to her parents, and told them all that had happened. There was now great joy and gladness over the whole kingdom, because the princess was saved, and because she had also set free her twelve brothers.

THE BEAR AND THE FOX

1. SLIP PINE-ROOT, GRIP FOX-FOOT

ONCE upon a time there was a bear, who sat on a sunny hill-side taking a nap. Just then a fox came slinking by and saw him.

"Aha! Have I caught you napping, grandfather? See if I don't play you a trick this time!" said Reynard to himself.

He then found three wood-mice and laid them on a stump of a tree just under the bear's nose.

"Boo! Bruin! Peter the hunter is just behind that stump!" shouted the fox right into the bear's ear, and then took to his heels and made off into the wood.

The bear woke at once, and when he saw the three mice he became so angry that he lifted his paw and was just going to strike them, for he thought it was they who had shouted in his ear.

But just then he saw Reynard's tail between the bushes, and he set off at such a speed that the branches crackled under him, and Bruin was soon so close upon Reynard that he caught him by the right hind leg just as he was running into a hole under a pine-tree.

Reynard was now in a fix; but he was not to be outwitted, and he cried:

"Slip pine-root, grip fox-foot," and so the bear let go his hold; but the fox laughed far down in the hole, and said:

"I sold you that time, also, grandfather!"

"Out of sight is not out of mind!" said the bear, who was in a fine fury.

2. THE BEAR AND THE FOX MAKE A WAGER

The other morning, when Bruin came trudging across the moor with a fat pig, Master Reynard was lying on a stone by the moor-side.

"Good day, grandfather!" said the fox. "What nice thing have you got there?"

"Pork," said the bear.

"I have got something tasty as well," said the fox.

"What's that?" said the bear.

"It's the biggest bees' nest I ever found," said Reynard.

"Ah, indeed," said the bear grinning, and his mouth began to water; he thought a little honey would be so nice. "Shall we change victuals?" he said.

"No, I won't do that," said Reynard. But they made a wager about naming three kinds of trees. If the fox could say them quicker than the bear, he was to have one bite at the pig; but if the bear could say them quicker, he was to have one suck at the bees' nest. The bear thought he would be able to suck all the honey up at one gulp.

"Well," said the fox, "that's all well and good, but if I win you must promise to tear off the bristles where I want to have a bite," he said.

"Well I suppose I must, since you are too lazy yourself;" said the bear.

Then they began to name the trees:

"Spruce, fir, pine," growled the bear. His voice was very gruff. But all these were only different names of one kind of tree.

"Ash, aspen, oak," screeched the fox, so that the forest resounded. He had thus won the bet, and so he jumped down, took the heart out of the pig at one bite and tried to run off. But the bear was angry, because he had taken the best bit of the whole pig, and seized hold of him by his tail and held him fast.

"Just wait a bit," said the bear, who was furious.

"Never mind, grandfather; if you'll let me go, you shall have a taste of my honey," said the fox.

When the bear heard this, he let go his hold and the fox jumped up on the stone after the honey.

"Over this nest," said Reynard, "I'll put a leaf, and in the leaf there is a hole, through which you can suck the honey." He then put the nest right up under the bear's nose, pulled away the leaf, jumped on to the stone, and began grinning and laughing; for there was neither honey nor honeycomb in the nest. It was a wasps' nest, as big as a man's head, full of wasps, and out they swarmed and stung the bear in his eyes and ears and on his mouth and snout. He had so much to do with scratching them off him, that he had no time to think of Reynard.

Ever since the bear has been afraid of wasps.

3. THE BEAR AND THE FOX GO INTO PARTNERSHIP

Once the fox and the bear made up their minds to have a field in common. They found a small clearing far away in the forest, where they sowed rye the first year.

"WHAT NICE THING HAVE YOU GOT THERE?" ASKED THE FOX. "PORK," SAID THE BEAR

"Now we must share and share alike," said Reynard; "if you will have the roots, I will have the tops," he said.

Yes, Bruin was quite willing; but when they had thrashed the crop, the fox got all the corn, while the bear got nothing but the roots and tares.

Bruin didn't like this, but the fox said it was only as they had agreed.

"This year I am the gainer," said the fox; "another year it will be your turn; you can then have the tops and I will be satisfied with the roots."

Next spring the fox asked the bear if he didn't think turnips would be the right thing for that year.

"Yes, that's better food than corn," said the bear; and the fox thought the same.

When the autumn came the fox took the turnips, but the bear only got the tops.

The bear then became so angry that he parted company then and there with Reynard.

4. REYNARD WANTS TO TASTE HORSEFLESH

One day the bear was lying eating a horse, which he had killed. Reynard was about again and came slinking along, his mouth watering for a tasty bit of the horse-flesh.

He sneaked in and out and round about till he came up behind the bear, when he made a spring to the other side of the carcase, snatching a piece as he jumped across.

The bear was not slow either; he made a dash after Reynard and caught the tip of his red tail in his paw. Since that time the fox has always had a white tip to his tail.

"Wait a bit, Reynard, and come here," said the bear, "and I'll teach you how to catch horses."

Yes, Reynard was quite willing to learn that, but he didn't trust himself too near the bear.

"When you see a horse lying asleep in a sunny place," said the bear, "you must tie yourself fast with the hair of his tail to your brush, and then fasten your teeth in his thigh," he said.

Before long the fox found a horse lying asleep on a sunny hillside; and so he did as the bear had told him; he knotted and tied himself well to the horse with the hair of the tail and then fastened his teeth into his thigh.

Up jumped the horse and began to kick and gallop, so that Reynard was dashed against stock and stone, and was so bruised and battered, that he nearly lost his senses.

All at once a hare rushed by. "Where are you off to in such a hurry, Reynard?" said the hare.

"I'm having a ride, Bunny!" said the fox.

The hare sat up on his hind legs and laughed till the sides of his mouth split right up to his ears, at the thought of Reynard having such a grand ride; but since then the fox has never thought of catching horses again.

That time it was Bruin who for once had the better of Reynard; otherwise they say the bear is as simple-minded as the trolls.

THE COCK WHO FELL INTO THE BREWING-VAT

Once upon a time there was a cock and a hen, who were out in a field scratching and scraping and pecking.

All at once the hen found a barleycorn, and the cock found a bur of hops, and so they made up their minds they would make some malt and brew beer for Christmas.

"I plucked the barley and I malted the corn and brewed the beer, and the beer is good," cackled the hen.

"Is the wort strong enough?" said the cock, and flew up to the edge of the vat to taste it; but when he stooped down to take a sip, he began flapping with his wings and fell on his head into the vat and was drowned.

When the hen saw this, she was quite beside herself; she flew on to the hearth and began to scream and cry:

"Got, got, got, drowned! got, got, got, drowned!" and this she went on crying all the time and would not stop.

"What is the matter with you, Mother Tup, since you are crying and grieving so?" asked the hand-quern.

"Oh, Father Tup has fallen into the brewing-vat and got drowned and there he lies dead!" said the hen; "that's the reason I cry and grieve."

"Well, if I can't do anything else, I will grind and groan," said the hand-quern, and began grinding as fast as it could.

When the stool heard this, it said:

"What's the matter with you, quern, since you groan and grind so fast?"

"Oh, Father Tup has fallen into the brewing-vat and got drowned; Mother Tup is sitting on the hearth, crying and grieving; therefore I grind and groan," said the hand-quern.

"Well, if I can't do anything else I shall creak," said the stool, and began creaking and cracking.

This the door heard, so it said:

"What's the matter with you? Why are you creaking, stool?"

"Oh, Father Tup has fallen into the brewing-vat and got drowned; Mother Tup is sitting on the hearth crying and grieving, and the hand-quern is grinding and groaning; therefore I creak and crack and crackle," said the stool.

"Well, if I can't do anything else, I'll bang and slam and whine and whistle," said the door, and began opening and shutting and slamming and banging till it went through one's bones and marrow to hear it.

This the dust-bin heard.

"Why are you slamming and banging like that, door?" said the bin.

"Oh, Father Tup fell into the brewing-vat and got drowned;

Mother Tup is sitting on the hearth crying and grieving; the hand-quern is grinding and groaning; the stool is creaking and cracking; therefore I keep slamming and banging," said the door.

"Well, if I can't do anything else, I'll fume and smoke," said the dust-bin, and began fuming and smoking, and sending the dust up in clouds all over the room.

This the hay-rake saw, as it stood peeping in through the window.

"Why are you raising the dust like that, dust-bin?" asked the rake.

"Oh, Father Tup fell into the brewing-vat and got drowned; Mother Tup is sitting on the hearth crying and grieving, the hand-quern is grinding and groaning, the stool is creaking and cracking; the door is slamming and banging; therefore I keep fuming and smoking," said the dust-bin.

"Well, if I can't do anything else, I'll rake and rend," said the rake, and began rending and raking.

This the aspen-tree saw, as it looked on.

"Why do you rend and rake like that, rake?" said the tree.

"Oh, Father Tup fell into the brewing-vat and got drowned; Mother Tup is sitting on the hearth crying and grieving; the hand-quern is grinding and groaning; the stool is creaking and cracking; the door is slamming and banging; the dust-bin is fuming and smoking; therefore I keep rending and raking," said the rake.

"Well, if I can't do anything else," said the aspen, "I will quiver and quake."

This the birds noticed. "Why do you quiver and quake like that?" said the birds to the tree.

"Oh, Father Tup fell into the brewing-vat and got drowned; Mother Tup is sitting on the hearth crying and grieving; the hand-quern is grinding and groaning; the stool is creaking and

THE MAN BEGAN PULLING THE BESOM TO PIECES, AND HIS WIFE TOOK ONE LADLEFUL OF PORRIDGE AFTER ANOTHER AND DAUBED IT ALL OVER THE PLACE

cracking; the door is slamming and banging; the dust-bin is fuming and smoking; the rake is rending and raking; therefore I quiver and quake," said the aspen.

"Well, if we can't do anything else we will pluck off our feathers," said the birds, and began pecking and plucking till the feathers flew about the farm like snow.

The farmer stood looking on, and when he saw the feathers flying about he asked the birds:

"Why are you plucking off your feathers like that, birds?"

"Oh, Father Tup fell into the brewing-vat and got drowned; Mother Tup is sitting on the hearth crying and grieving; the hand-quern is grinding and groaning; the stool is creaking and cracking; the door is slamming and banging; the dust-bin is fuming and smoking; the rake is rending and raking; the aspen is quivering and quaking: therefore we keep pecking and plucking," said the birds.

"Well, if I can't do anything else I will pull the besoms to pieces," said the farmer, and began tugging and pulling the besoms to pieces, so that the twigs flew about, both east and west.

His wife was boiling the porridge for supper when she saw this.

"Why are you pulling the besoms to pieces, husband?" said she.

"Oh, Father Tup fell into the brewing-vat and got drowned; Mother Tup is sitting on the hearth crying and grieving; the hand-quern is grinding and groaning; the stool is creaking and creaking; the door is slamming and banging; the dust-bin is fuming and smoking; the rake is rending and raking; the aspen is quivering and quaking; the birds are pecking and plucking off their feathers: therefore I am pulling the besom to pieces," said the man.

"Well, then, I'll daub the walls all over with porridge," she said. And she set about it there and then, and took one ladleful after another and smeared the porridge all over the walls, so that no one could see what they were made of.

Then they kept the burial feast of the cock who fell into the brewing-vat. And if you don't believe it, you had better go there and taste both the beer and the porridge.

THE COCK AND THE FOX

There was once a cock who stood on a dunghill, crowing and flapping his wings.

A fox just then came strolling by.

"Good-day," said the fox; "that's a very fine crow, but can you stand on one leg and crow with your eyes shut, as your father did?"

"I can easily do that," said the cock, and stood on one leg and crowed. But he only shut one eye, and then he strutted about flapping his wings as if he had done something grand.

"That was very nice," said the fox; "almost as nice as when the parson chants in church; but can you stand on one leg and crow with both your eyes shut at the same time? I scarcely think you can," said Reynard. "No; that father of yours, he was really wonderful."

"Oh, I can do that as well," said the cock, and began to crow standing on one leg and closing both his eyes, when all of a sudden the fox made a dash at him, caught him by the neck, and slung him across his back, and before he had finished his crow Reynard had set off with him for the forest as quickly as he could.

When they got under an old pine-tree Reynard threw the cock down, put his paw on his breast, and was going to help himself to a tasty bit.

"You are not so pious as your father, Reynard," said the cock: "he always crossed himself and said grace before his meals."

Reynard thought he ought to show a little piety, so he let go his hold and was just going to say grace when up flew the cock and settled in the tree above.

"I'll be even with you yet," said the fox to himself and went off. He soon returned with a couple of chippings which the woodcutters had left behind.

The cock kept peeping and peering to see what it could be.

"What have you got there?" he said.

"Oh, some letters I have got from the Pope in Rome," said the fox. "Won't you help me to read them, for I am getting rather shortsighted myself?"

"I would with pleasure, but I dare not just now," said the

cock; "there is a man coming along with a gun; I see him from behind the tree—I see him!"

When the fox heard the cock prating about a man with a gun he took to his heels as fast as he could.

That time it was the cock who outwitted Reynard.

THE THREE PRINCESSES IN THE BLUE MOUNTAIN

There were once upon a time a king and queen who had no children, and they took it so much to heart that they hardly ever had a happy moment. One day the king stood in the portico and looked out over the big meadows and all that was his. But he felt he could have no enjoyment out of it all, since he did not know what would become of it after his time. As he stood there pondering, an old beggar woman came up to him and asked him for a trifle in heaven's name. She greeted him and curtsied, and asked what ailed the king, since he looked so sad.

"You can't do anything to help me, my good woman," said the king; "it's no use telling you."

"I am not so sure about that," said the beggar woman. "Very little is wanted when luck is in the way. The king is thinking that he has no heir to his crown and kingdom, but he need not mourn on that account," she said. "The queen shall have three daughters, but great care must be taken that they do not come out under the open heavens before they are all fifteen years old; otherwise a snowdrift will come and carry them away."

When the time came the queen had a beautiful baby girl; the year after she had another, and the third year she also had a girl.

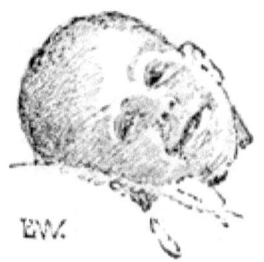

The king and queen were glad beyond all measure; but although the king was very happy, he did not forget to set a watch at the palace door, so that the princesses should not get out.

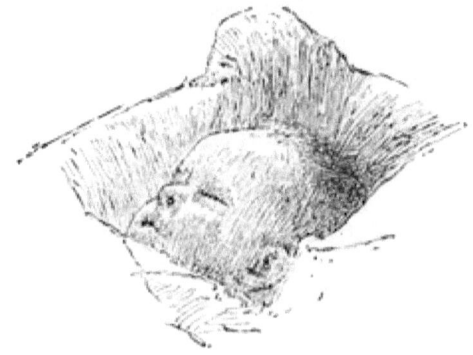

As they grew up they became both fair and beautiful, and all went well with them in every way. Their only sorrow was that they were not allowed to go out and play like other children. For all they begged and prayed their parents, and for all they besought the sentinel, it was of no avail; go out they must not before they were fifteen years old, all of them.

So one day, not long before the fifteenth birthday of the youngest princess, the king and the queen were out driving, and the princesses were standing at the window and looking out. The sun was shining, and everything looked so green and beautiful that they felt they must go out, happen what might. So they begged and entreated and urged the sentinel, all three of them, that he should let them down into the garden. "He could see for himself how warm and pleasant it was; no snowy weather could come on such a day." Well, he didn't think it looked much like it either, and if they must go they had better go, the soldier said; but it must only be for a minute, and he himself would go with them and look after them.

When they got down into the garden they ran up and down, and filled their laps with flowers and green leaves, the prettiest they could find. At last they could manage no more, but just as they were going indoors they caught sight of a large rose at the other end of the garden. It was many times prettier than any they had gathered, so they must have that also. But just as they bent down to take the rose a big dense snowdrift came and carried them away.

There was great mourning over the whole country, and the king made known from all the churches that any one who could save the princesses should have half the kingdom and his golden crown and whichever princess he liked to choose.

You can well understand there were plenty who wanted to gain half the kingdom, and a princess into the bargain; so there were people of both high and low degree who set out for all parts of the country. But there was no one who could find the princesses, or even get any tidings of them.

When all the grand and rich people in the country had had their turn, a captain and a lieutenant came to the palace, and wanted to try their luck. The king fitted them out both with silver and gold, and wished them success on their journey.

Then came a soldier, who lived with his mother in a little cottage some way from the palace. He had dreamt one night that he also was trying to find the princesses. When the morning came he still remembered what he had dreamt, and told his mother about it.

"Some witchery must have got hold of you," said the woman, "but you must dream the same thing three nights running, else there is nothing in it." And the next two nights the same thing happened; he had the same dream, and he felt he must go. So he washed himself and put on his uniform, and went into the kitchen at the palace. It was the day after the captain and the lieutenant had set out.

"You had better go home again," said the king, "the princesses are beyond your reach, I should say; and besides I have

THE SOLDIER'S MOTHER LIVED IN A LITTLE COTTAGE.

spent so much money on outfits that I have nothing left to-day. You had better come back another time."

"If I go, I must go to-day," said the soldier. "Money I do not want; I only need a drop in my flask and some food in my wallet," he said; "but it must be a good walletful—as much meat and bacon as I can carry."

Yes, that he might have if that was all he wanted.

So he set off, and he had not gone many miles before he overtook the captain and the lieutenant.

"Where are you going?" asked the captain, when he saw the man in uniform.

THE PRINCESSES BEGGED AND ENTREATED THE SENTINEL TO LET THEM DOWN INTO THE GARDEN

"I am going to try if I can find the princesses," answered the soldier.

"So are we," said the captain, "and since your errand is the same you may keep company with us, for if we don't find them, you are not likely to find them either, my lad," said he.

When they had gone awhile the soldier left the high road, and took a path into the forest.

"Where are you going?" said the captain; "it is best to follow the high road."

"That may be," said the soldier, "but this is my way."

He kept to the path, and when the others saw this they turned round and followed him. Away they went further and further, far across big moors and along narrow valleys.

At last it became lighter, and when they had got out of the forest altogether they came to a long bridge, which they had to cross. But on that bridge a bear stood on guard. He rose on his hind legs and came towards them, as if he wanted to eat them.

"What shall we do now?" said the captain.

"They say that the bear is fond of meat," said the soldier, and then he threw a fore quarter to him, and so they got past. But when they reached the other end of the bridge, they saw a lion which came roaring towards them with open jaws as if he wanted to swallow them.

"I think we had better turn to right-about, we shall never be able to get past him alive," said the captain.

"Oh, I don't think he is so very dangerous," said the soldier; "I have heard that lions are very fond of bacon, and I have half a pig in my wallet:" and then he threw a ham to the lion, who began eating and gnawing, and thus they got past him also.

In the evening they came to a fine big house. Each room was more gorgeous than the other; all was glitter and splendour wherever they looked; but that did not satisfy their hunger. The captain and the lieutenant went round rattling their money, and wanted to buy some food; but they saw no people nor could they find a crumb of anything in the house, so the soldier offered them some food from his wallet, which they were not too proud to accept, nor did they want any pressing. They helped themselves of what he had as if they had never tasted food before.

The next day the captain said they would have to go out shooting and try to get something to live upon. Close to the house was a large forest where there were plenty of hares and birds. The lieutenant was to remain at home and cook the remainder of the food in the soldier's wallet. In the meantime the

IN THE EVENING THEY CAME TO A BIG FINE HOUSE.

captain and the soldier shot so much game that they were hardly able to carry it home. When they came to the door they found the lieutenant in such a terrible plight that he was scarcely able to open the door to them.

"What is the matter with you?" said the captain. The lieutenant then told them that as soon as they were gone, a tiny, little man with a long beard, who went on crutches, came in and asked so plaintively for a penny; but no sooner had he got it than he let it fall on the floor, and for all he raked and scraped with his crutch he was not able to get hold of it, so stiff and stark was he.

"I pitied the poor, old body," said the lieutenant, "and so I bent down to pick up the penny, but then he was neither stiff nor stark any longer. He began to belabour me with his crutches till very soon I was unable to move a limb."

"You ought to be ashamed of yourself! you, one of the king's officers, to let an old cripple give you a thrashing, and then tell people of it into the bargain!" said the captain. "Pshaw! to-morrow I'll stop at home and then you'll hear another story."

The next day the lieutenant and the soldier went out shooting and the captain remained at home to do the cooking and look after the house. But if he fared no worse, he certainly fared no better than the lieutenant. In a little while the old man came in and asked for a penny. He let it fall as soon as he got it; gone it was and could not be found. So he asked the captain to help him to find it, and the captain, without giving a thought, bent down to look for it. But no sooner was he on his knees than the cripple began belabouring him with his crutches, and every time the captain tried to rise, he got a blow which sent him reeling. When the others came home in the evening, he still lay on the same spot and could neither see nor speak.

The third day the soldier was to remain at home, while the other two went out shooting. The captain said he must take care of himself, "For the old fellow will soon put an end to you, my lad," said he.

"Oh, there can't be much life in one if such an old crook can take it," said the soldier.

They were no sooner outside the door, than the old man came in and asked for a penny again.

"Money I have never owned," said the soldier, "but food I'll give you, as soon as it is ready," said he, "but if we are to get it cooked, you must go and cut the wood."

"That I can't," said the old man.

"If you can't, you must learn," said the soldier. "I will soon show you. Come along with me down to the wood-shed." There he dragged out a heavy log and cut a cleft in it, and drove in a wedge till the cleft deepened.

"Now you must lie down and look right along the cleft, and you'll soon learn how to cut wood," said the soldier. "In the meantime I'll show you how to use the axe."

The old man was not sufficiently cunning and did as he was

told; he lay down and looked steadily along the log. When the soldier saw that the old man's beard had got well into the cleft, he struck out the wedge; the cleft closed and the old man was caught by the beard. The soldier began to beat him with the axe handle, and then swung the axe round his head, and vowed that he would split his skull if he did not tell him, there and then, where the princesses were.

"Spare my life, spare my life, and I'll tell you!" said the old man. "To the east of the house there is a big mound; on top of the mound you must dig out a square piece of turf, and then you will see a big stone slab. Under that there is a deep hole through which you must let yourself down, and you'll then come to another world where you will find the princesses. But the way is long and dark and it goes both through fire and water."

When the soldier got to know this, he released the old man, who was not long in making off.

When the captain and lieutenant came home they were surprised to find the soldier alive. He told them what had happened from first to last, where the princesses were and how they should find them. They became as pleased as if they had already found them, and when they had had some food, they took with them a basket and as much rope as they could find, and all three set off to the mound. There they first dug out the turf just as the old man had told them, and underneath they found a big stone slab, which it took all their strength to turn over. They then began to measure how deep it was; they joined on ropes both two and three times, but they were no nearer the bottom the last time than the first. At last they had to join all the ropes they had, both the coarse and fine, and then they found it reached the bottom.

The captain was, of course, the first who wanted to descend; "But when I tug at the rope you must make haste to drag me up again," he said. He found the way both dark and unpleasant, but he thought he would go on as long as it became no worse. But all at once he felt ice cold water spouting about his ears; he became frightened to death and began tugging at the rope.

THE LITTLE OLD MAN BEGAN BELABOURING THE LIEUTENANT WITH HIS CRUTCHES TILL HE WAS UNABLE TO MOVE A LIMB

The lieutenant was the next to try, but it fared no better with him. No sooner had he got through the flood of water than he saw a blazing fire yawning beneath him, which so frightened him that he also turned back.

The soldier then got into the bucket, and down he went through fire and water, right on till he came to the bottom, where it was so pitch dark that he could not see his hand before him. He dared not let go the basket, but went round in a circle, feeling and fumbling about him. At last he discovered a gleam of light far, far away like the dawn of day, and he went on in that direction.

When he had gone a bit it began to grow light around him, and before long he saw a golden sun rising in the sky and everything around him became as bright and beautiful as if in a fairy world.

First he came to some cattle, which were so fat that their hides glistened a long way off, and when he had got past them he came to a fine, big palace. He walked through many rooms without meeting anybody. At last he heard the hum of a spinning wheel, and when he entered the room he found the eldest princess sitting there spinning copper yarn; the room and everything in it was of brightly polished copper.

"Oh dear, oh dear! what are Christian people doing here?" said the princess. "Heaven preserve you! what do you want?"

"I want to set you free and get you out of the mountain," said the soldier.

"Pray do not stay. If the troll comes home he will put an end to you at once; he has three heads," said she.

"I do not care if he has four," said the soldier. "I am here, and here I shall remain."

"Well, if you will be so headstrong, I must see if I can help you," said the princess.

She then told him to creep behind the big brewing-vat which stood in the front hall; meanwhile she would receive the troll and scratch his heads till he went to sleep.

"And when I go out and call the hens you must make haste and come in," she said. "But you must first try if you can swing the sword which is lying on the table." No, it was too heavy, he could not even move it. He had then to take a strengthening draught from the horn, which hung behind the door; after that he was just able to stir it, so he took another draught and then he could lift it. At last he took a right, big draught and he could swing the sword as easily as anything.

All at once the troll came home; he walked so heavily that the palace shook.

"Ugh, ugh! I smell Christian flesh and blood in my house," said he.

"Yes," answered the princess, "a raven flew past here just now and in his beak he had a human bone, which he dropped down the chimney; I threw it out and swept and cleaned up after it, but I suppose it still smells."

"So it does," said the troll.

"But come and lie down and I'll scratch your heads," said the princess; "the smell will be gone by the time you wake."

The troll was quite willing, and before long he fell asleep and began snoring. When she saw he was sleeping soundly she placed some stools and cushions under his heads and went to call the hens. The soldier then stole into the room with the sword and with one blow cut all the three heads off the troll.

The princess was as pleased as a fiddler, and went with the soldier to her sisters, so that he could also set them free. First of all they went across a courtyard and then through many long rooms till they came to a big door.

"Here you must enter; here she is," said the princess. When he opened the door he found himself in a large hall, where everything was of pure silver; there sat the second sister at a silver spinning-wheel.

"Oh, dear; oh, dear!" she said. "What do you want here?"

"I want to set you free from the troll," said the soldier.

"Pray do not stay, but go," said the princess. "If he finds you here he will take your life on the spot."

"That would be awkward—that is if I don't take his first," said the soldier.

"Well, since you will stay," she said; "you will have to creep behind the big brewing-vat in the front hall. But you must make haste and come as soon as you hear me calling the hens."

First of all he had to try if he was able to swing the troll's sword, which lay on the table; it was much larger and heavier than the first one; he was hardly able to move it. He then took three draughts from the horn and he could then lift it, and when he had taken three more he could handle it as if it were a rolling-pin.

Shortly afterwards he heard a heavy, rumbling noise that was quite terrible, and directly afterwards a troll with six heads came in.

"Ugh, ugh!" he said as soon as he got his noses inside the door. "I smell Christian blood and bone in my house."

"Yes, just think! A raven came flying past here with a thigh-bone, which he dropped down the chimney," said the princess. "I threw it out, but the raven brought it back again. At last I got rid of it and made haste to clean the room, but I suppose the smell is not quite gone," she said.

"No, I can smell it well," said the troll; but he was tired and put his heads in the princess's lap and she went on scratching them till they all fell a-snoring. Then she called the hens, and the soldier came and cut off all the six heads as if they were set on cabbage stalks.

She was no less glad than her eldest sister, as you may imagine, and danced and sang; but in the midst of their joy they remembered their youngest sister. They went with the soldier across a large courtyard and after walking through many, many rooms he came to the hall of gold, where the third sister was.

She sat at a golden spinning-wheel spinning gold yarn, and

the room from ceiling to floor glistened and glittered till it hurt one's eyes.

"Heaven preserve both you and me, what do you want here?" said the princess. "Go, go, else the troll will kill us both."

"Just as well two as one," answered the soldier. The princess cried and wept; but it was all of no use, he must and would remain. Since there was no help for it he would have to try if he could use the troll's sword on the table in the front hall. But he was only just able to move it; it was still larger and heavier than the other two swords.

He then had to take the horn down from the wall and take three draughts from it, but was only just able to stir the sword. When he had taken three more draughts he could lift it, and when he had taken another three he swung it as easily as if it had been a feather.

The princess then settled with the soldier to do the same as her sisters had done. As soon as the troll was well asleep she would call the hens, and he must then make haste and come in and put an end to the troll.

All of a sudden they heard such a thundering, rambling noise, as if the walls and roof were tumbling in.

"Ugh! Ugh! I smell Christian blood and bone in my house," said the troll sniffing with all his nine noses.

"Yes, you never saw the like! Just now a raven flew past here and dropped a human bone down the chimney. I threw it out, but the raven brought it back and this went on for some time," said the princess; but she got it buried at last, she said, and she had both swept and cleaned the place, but she supposed it still smelt.

"Yes, I can smell it well," said the troll.

"Come here and lie down in my lap and I will scratch your heads," said the princess. "The smell will be all gone when you awake."

He did so, and when he was snoring at his best she put stools and cushions under the heads so that she could get away to call the hens. The soldier then came in in his stockinged feet and struck at the troll, so that eight of the heads fell off at one blow. But the sword was too short and did not reach far enough; the ninth head woke up and began to roar.

"Ugh! Ugh! I smell a Christian."

"Yes, here he is," answered the soldier, and before the troll could get up and seize hold of him the soldier struck him another blow and the last head rolled along the floor.

You can well imagine how glad the princesses became now that they no longer had to sit and scratch the trolls' heads; they did not know how they could do enough for him who had saved them. The youngest princess took off her gold ring and knotted it in his hair. They then took with them as much gold and silver as they thought they could carry and set off on their way home.

As soon as they tugged at the rope the captain and the lieutenant pulled up the princesses, the one after the other. But when they were safely up the soldier thought it was foolish of him not to have gone up before the princesses, for he had not very much belief in his comrades. He thought he would first try them, so he put a heavy lump of gold in the basket and got out of the way. When the basket was half-way up they cut the rope and the lump of gold fell to the bottom with such a crash that the pieces flew about his ears.

"Now we are rid of him," they said, and threatened the princesses with their life if they did not say that it was they who had saved them from the trolls. They were forced to agree to this, much against their will, and especially the youngest princess; but life was precious, and so the two who were strongest had their way.

When the captain and lieutenant got home with the princesses you may be sure there were great rejoicings at the palace. The king was so glad he didn't know which leg to stand on; he brought out his best wine from his cupboard and wished the two officers welcome. If they had never been honoured before they were honoured now in full measure, and no mistake. They walked and strutted about the whole of the day, as if they were the cocks of the walk, since they were now going to have the king for father-in-law. For it was understood they should each have whichever of the princesses they liked and half the kingdom between them. They both wanted the youngest princess, but for all they prayed and threatened her it was of no use; she would not hear or listen to either.

They then asked the king if they might have twelve men to watch over her; she was so sad and melancholy since she had been in the mountain that they were afraid she might do something to herself.

Yes, that they might have, and the king himself told the watch they must look well after her and follow her wherever she went and stood.

They then began to prepare for the wedding of the two eldest sisters; it should be such a wedding as never was heard or spoken of before, and there was no end to the brewing and the baking and the slaughtering.

In the meantime the soldier walked and strolled about down in the other world. He thought it was hard that he should see neither people nor daylight any more; but he would have to do something, he thought, and so for many days he went about from room to room and opened all the drawers and cupboards and searched about on the shelves and looked at all the fine things that were there. At last he came to a drawer in a table, in which there lay a golden key; he tried this key to all the locks he could find, but there was none it fitted till he came to a little cupboard over the bed, and in that he found an old rusty whistle. "I wonder if there is any sound in it," he thought, and put it to his mouth. No sooner had he whistled than he heard a whizzing and a whirring from all quarters, and such a large flock of birds swept down, that they blackened all the field in which they settled.

"What does our master want to-day?" they asked.

If he were their master, the soldier said, he would like to know if they could tell him how to get up to the earth again. No, none of them knew anything about that ; "But our mother has not yet arrived," they said ; "if she can't help you, no one can."

So he whistled once more, and shortly heard something flapping its wings far away, and then it began to blow so hard that he was carried away between the houses like a wisp of hay across the courtyard, and if he had not caught hold of the fence he would no doubt have been blown away altogether.

A big eagle—bigger than you can imagine—then swooped down in front of him.

"You come rather sharply," said the soldier.

"As you whistle so I come," answered the eagle. So he asked her if she knew any means by which he could get away from the world in which they were.

"You can't get away from here unless you can fly," said the eagle, "but if you will slaughter twelve oxen for me, so that I can have a really good meal, I will try and help you. Have you got a knife?"

"No, but I have a sword," he said. When the eagle had swallowed the twelve oxen she asked the soldier to kill one more for victuals on the journey. "Every time I gape you must be quick and fling a piece into my mouth," she said, "else I shall not be able to carry you up to earth."

He did as she asked him and hung two large bags of meat round her neck and seated himself among her feathers. The eagle then began to flap her wings and off they went through the air like the wind. It was as much as the soldier could do to hold on, and it was with the greatest difficulty he managed to throw the pieces of flesh into the eagle's mouth every time she opened it.

At last the day began to dawn, and the eagle was then almost exhausted and began flapping with her wings, but the soldier was prepared and seized the last hind quarter and flung it to her. Then she gained strength and brought him up to earth. When she had sat and rested a while at the top of a large pine-tree she set off with him again at such a pace that flashes of lightning were seen both by sea and land wherever they went.

Close to the palace the soldier got off and the eagle flew home again, but first she told him that if he at any time should want her he need only blow the whistle and she would be there at once.

In the meantime everything was ready at the palace, and the time approached when the captain and lieutenant were to be married with the two eldest princesses, who, however, were not much happier than their youngest sister; scarcely a day passed without weeping and mourning, and the nearer the wedding-day approached the more sorrowful did they become.

At last the king asked what was the matter with them; he thought it was very strange that they were not merry and happy now that they were saved and had been set free and were going to be married. They had to give some answer, and so the eldest sister said they never would be happy any more unless they could get such checkers as they had played with in the blue mountain.

That, thought the king, could be easily managed, and so he sent word to all the best and cleverest goldsmiths in the country that they should make these checkers for the princesses. For all they tried there was no one who could make them. At last all the goldsmiths had been to the palace except one, and he was an old, infirm man who had not done any work for many years except odd jobs, by which he was just able to keep himself alive. To him the soldier went and asked to be apprenticed. The old man was so glad to get him, for he had not had an apprentice for many a day, that he brought out a flask from his chest and sat down to drink with the soldier. Before long the drink got into his head, and when the soldier saw this he persuaded him to go up to the palace and tell the king that he would undertake to make the checkers for the princesses.

He was ready to do that on the spot; he had made finer and grander things in his day, he said. When the king heard there

THE OLD GOLDSMITH WENT TO THE PALACE AND TOLD THE KING HE WOULD
UNDERTAKE TO MAKE THE CHECKERS FOR THE PRINCESSES

was some one outside who could make the checkers he was not long in coming out.

"Is it true what you say, that you can make such checkers as my daughters want?" he asked.

"Yes, it is no lie," said the goldsmith; that he would answer for.

"That's well!" said the king. "Here is the gold to make them with; but if you do not succeed you will lose your life, since you have come and offered yourself, and they must be finished in three days."

The next morning when the goldsmith had slept off the effects of the drink, he was not quite so confident about the job. He wailed and wept and blew up his apprentice, who had got him into such a scrape while he was drunk. The best thing would be to make short work of himself at once, he said, for there could be no hope for his life; when the best and grandest goldsmiths could not make such checkers, was it likely that he could do it?

"Don't fret on that account," said the soldier, "but let me have the gold and I'll get the checkers ready in time; but I must have a room to myself to work in," he said. This he got, and thanks into the bargain.

The time wore on, and the soldier did nothing but lounge about, and the goldsmith began to grumble, because he would not begin with the work.

"Don't worry yourself about it," said the soldier, "there is plenty of time! If you are not satisfied with what I have promised you had better make them yourself." The same thing went on both that day and the next; and when the smith heard neither hammer nor file from the soldier's room the whole of the last day, he quite gave himself up for lost; it was now no use to think any longer about saving his life, he thought.

But when the night came on the soldier opened the window and blew his whistle. The eagle then came and asked what he wanted.

"Those gold checkers, which the princesses had in the blue

mountain," said the soldier; "but you'll want something to eat first, I suppose? I have two ox carcases lying ready for you in the hay-loft yonder; you had better finish them," he said. When the eagle had done she did not tarry, and long before the sun rose she was back again with the checkers. The soldier then put them under his bed and lay down to sleep.

Early next morning the goldsmith came and knocked at his door.

"What are you after now again?" asked the soldier. "You rush about enough in the day, goodness knows! If one cannot have peace when one is in bed, whoever would be an apprentice here?" said he.

Neither praying nor begging helped that time; the goldsmith must and would come in, and at last he was let in.

And then you may be sure, there was soon an end to his wailing.

But still more glad than the goldsmith were the princesses, when he came up to the palace with the checkers, and gladdest of all was the youngest princess.

"Have you made them yourself?" she asked.

"No, if I must speak the truth, it is not I," he said, "but my apprentice, who has made them."

"I should like to see that apprentice," said the princess. In fact all three wanted to see him, and if he valued his life, he would have to come.

He was not afraid, either of women-folk or grand-folk, said the soldier, and if it could be any amusement to them to look at his rags, they should soon have that pleasure.

The youngest princess recognised him at once; she pushed the soldiers aside and ran up to him, gave him her hand, and said:

"Good day, and many thanks for all you have done for us. It is he who freed us from the trolls in the mountain," she said to the king. "He is the one I will have!" and then she pulled off his cap and showed them the ring she had tied in his hair.

It soon came out how the captain and lieutenant had behaved,

"I HAVE TWO OX CARCASSES LYING READY FOR YOU IN THE HAY-LOFT YONDER," SAID THE SOLDIER TO THE EAGLE

THE THREE PRINCESSES IN THE BLUE MOUNTAIN 219

and so they had to pay the penalty of their treachery with their lives, and that was the end of their grandeur. But the soldier got the golden crown and half the kingdom, and married the youngest princess.

At the wedding they drank and feasted both well and long; for feast they all could, even if they could not find the princesses, and if they have not yet done feasting and drinking they must be at it still.

THE WORLD'S REWARD

There was once a man who went into the wood to cut trees for hurdles. But he did not find any which were as long and straight as he wanted them to be, till he got to a rocky place, where he heard groans and moans, as of some one in the pangs of death. So he went to see who it was that wanted help. He found that the groans came from under a big slab among the boulders. It was so heavy that it would take many men to lift it. But the man went into the wood and cut down a tree, which he used as a lever to lift the slab with. From under it there crawled a dragon, who then wanted to eat the man. But the man said he had saved the dragon's life, and it was base ingratitude to want to eat him.

"May be!" said the dragon. "But you can easily understand that I am hungry, having lain here a hundred years and tasted no food; besides, that is the reward one gets in the world."

The man begged and prayed for his life, and so they agreed that the first being they met should decide between them. If he was of a different opinion to the dragon the man should not lose his life, but if he thought the same as the dragon, the dragon should eat the man.

The first they met was an old dog, who was walking along the road under the hillside. They spoke to him and asked him to be their judge.

"Goodness only knows! I have served my master faithfully since I was a pup," said the dog; "I have watched many a night and many a time while he has been sound asleep, and I have saved the house and chattels from fire and thieves more than once; but now, when I can neither see nor hear any longer, he wants to shoot me; so I ran away, and I knock about from place to place, sniffing and begging my way till one day I shall die of hunger. No, that is the reward one gets in this world," said the dog.

"Then I'll eat you!" said the dragon, and was going to swallow the man; but the man spoke so well for himself, and begged so hard for his life, that the dragon agreed that the next being they met should decide between them; and if he said the same as the dragon and the dog, the dragon should eat him, and have a good meal of human flesh, but if not, the man should get off with his life.

An old horse then came dragging himself along the road just under the hillside. They spoke to him, and asked him to judge between them. Yes, that he would.

"Well, I have served my master as long as I was able to draw and carry," said the horse. "I have slaved and worked for him till the sweat streamed from every hair, and I have worked faithfully till I have become stiff and stark, and worn-out with work and age; now I am fit for nothing, and am not worth my keep, and so I am to have a bullet, says my master. No, that is the reward one gets in this world," said the horse.

"Then I'll eat you!" said the dragon, and opened its jaws wide to swallow the man. He again begged and prayed hard for his life, but the dragon said he wanted a mouthful of human flesh and was so hungry that he could not wait any longer.

"Look, there is some one coming, just as if he were sent to be our judge," said the man, as Reynard came slinking towards them between the boulders. "Good things come in threes," said the man; "let us ask him also, and if he judges like the others, you shall eat me on the spot."

"Very well," said the dragon. He had also heard that all good things came in threes, and so he would agree to that. The man spoke to the fox as he had done to the others.

"Yes, yes," said the fox; but he took the man aside.

"What will you give me, if I free you from the dragon?" he whispered in the man's ear.

"You shall come home with me and be lord and master over my fowls and geese every Thursday night," said the man.

"This is a case which can only be settled on the spot itself, my dear dragon," said the fox. "I cannot get into my head how such a large and mighty animal as yourself could find room under that slab"

"Well, I was lying up here sunning myself," said the dragon, "when an avalanche came down the mountain and turned the slab over me."

"That is very possible," said Reynard; "but I cannot understand it, nor will I believe it, till I see it," said he.

So the man said they had better try it, and the dragon slipped into the hole again, and just at that moment the man pulled away the lever, and the slab shut down the dragon again with a bang.

"You may now lie there till doomsday," said the fox, "since you had no pity on the man who saved you." The dragon yelled and groaned and prayed for himself, but the other two went their way.

The next Thursday evening the fox set out for the farm to help himself from the hen-roost, and hid himself behind a heap of poles, which were standing there. When the girl went to give the fowls their food, Reynard sneaked in, so that she did not notice him; and no sooner was she gone than he killed enough for eight days, and ate till he could not move. When the girl came back in the morning, the fox lay sleeping and snoring in the morning sunshine, with all his four legs stretched out; he was as sleek and round as a big sausage.

The girl ran to fetch her mistress, and she and all the others came back with sticks and poles, and began thrashing Reynard till

"THIS IS A CASE WHICH CAN ONLY BE SETTLED ON THE SPOT ITSELF,
MY DEAR DRAGON," SAID THE FOX

they almost killed him ; but at last when they thought they had done for him, Reynard found a hole in the floor, through which he slipped out and set off limping towards the wood.

"Oh dear, oh dear!" said Reynard ; " but I suppose that is the reward one gets in this world!"

THE COMPANION

There was once upon a time a peasant lad, who dreamt he was going to marry a princess far away in a strange country, and she was as red and white as milk and blood, and so rich that there was no end to her riches. When he awoke, he thought she still stood alive before him, and she was so sweet and beautiful that he felt he could not exist if he did not get her; so he sold what he had and set out in the world to find her.

He went far and further than far, and in the winter he came to a country where all the high roads were straight and had no turnings. When he had walked straight on for a quarter of a year, he came to a town, and outside the church door there lay a large block of ice in which stood a dead body; and all the people who were on their way to church spat on it as they passed it. The lad wondered at this, and when the parson came out of the church, he asked him what it all meant.

"He was a great evil-doer," said the parson, "and was punished for his ungodliness, and has been set up there to be mocked and scoffed at."

"What did he do?" asked the lad.

"When he was alive, he was a vintner," said the parson, "and he mixed his wine with water." The lad did not think this a very wicked deed; "and when he has paid for it with his life,"

WHEN THE PARSON CAME OUT OF THE CHURCH, THE LAD ASKED HIM WHAT IT ALL MEANT

said he, "they might as well let him lie in Christian ground and leave him in peace after death." But the parson said that could not be permitted on any account, for they would have to get people to break him out of the ice; and money would be wanted to buy burial ground from the church, the grave-digger would want payment for the grave, the owner of the church for the bells, the clerk for the singing, and the parson for casting earth on the coffin.

"Do you think there is anybody who will pay all this for an executed sinner?" he asked.

"Yes," said the lad. If he could only get him underground, he would pay all the funeral expenses out of the little he had.

The parson was still unwilling to bury him; but when the lad came with two men, and asked him in their presence to perform the ceremony, he answered that he dared not refuse. So they broke the vintner out of his block of ice and put him in Christian ground; they tolled the bells, and sang over him, and the parson cast the earth upon the coffin, and they drank of the funeral ale till they both cried and laughed. When the lad had paid all the expenses he had not many pennies left in his pocket.

He set out on the road again. But he had not gone far, before a man came after him and asked him if he did not think it was lonely to be travelling by himself.

No, the lad did not find it lonely for he had always something to think about, he said.

The man then asked if he did not want a servant.

"No," said the lad, "I am accustomed to be my own servant, and therefore I do not want any; but if I wanted one ever so much, I could not afford to have one, for I have no money to pay for his food or wages."

"You want a servant; that I know better than you," said the man, "and you will want one you can rely upon in life and death. If you will not have me as your servant you can take me as a companion. I promise you, that you will find me useful and it shall not cost you a penny. I'll pay my own way, and food and clothing you need not trouble about."

Well, on those terms he would willingly have him for a companion, and after that they travelled together, the man mostly going on in front and showing him the way. When they had travelled a long way over hills and dales through many countries they came to a mountain that lay across the road.

There the companion knocked and asked them to open. The rock opened for them, and when they came far into the mountain a troll woman came and offered them a stool.

"Won't you take a seat? You must be tired," she said.

"Take a seat yourself," said the man. So she had to sit down; but when she had done so, she stuck fast to the stool, for it was such that it did not let go anything that came near it. In the meantime they walked about inside the mountain and the companion looked around him till he saw a sword which hung over the door.

He wanted this very much, and if he could have it he promised the troll woman that he would let her loose.

"No," she cried, "ask me for anything else! You can have everything but that, for it is my Three-Sister-Sword!" There were three sisters who owned it together.

"Well, then you must sit there till the end of the world," said the man; but when she heard this she said that he could have it if he would set her free. So he took the sword and went away with it, but he left her sitting on the stool all the same.

When they had gone far across some bare mountains and broad hills, they came to another mountain that lay across the road. There the companion knocked and asked them to open. It happened as before; the rock opened for them and when they got far into the mountain there came a troll woman with a stool and asked them to sit down; they might be tired, she said.

"Sit down yourself," said the companion; and she fared just as her sister had fared. When she sat down on the stool, she stuck fast to it. In the meantime the lad and the companion walked about inside the mountain and the companion opened all the cupboards and drawers till he found what he searched for. It was a ball of gold yarn. He wanted this very much, and he promised the troll woman that if she would give it him he would let her loose. She said he could have all she possessed, but she would not part with that for it was her Three-Sister-Ball. But when she heard that she would have to sit there till the day of judgment if he did not get it, she said he might take it after all if only he would set her free. The companion took the ball, but he let her sit where she was.

So they went for many days over hills and through forests, till they came to a mountain that lay across the road. The same thing happened as before; the companion knocked, the rock opened, and inside the mountain a troll woman came with a stool and asked them to sit down, for they might be tired.

But the companion said, "Sit down yourself!" and there she sat. They had not gone through many rooms before the companion saw an old hat, which hung on a peg behind the door. He wanted that very much, but the troll woman did not want to part with it, for it was her Three-Sister-Hat, and if she gave it away she would be most unhappy. But when she heard that she would have to sit there till the end of the world if he did not get it, she said he might take it if he only let her loose. No sooner had the companion got the hat than he told her to remain sitting where she was, just like her sisters.

After a long time they came to a fjord. Then the companion took the ball of gold yarn, and threw it so hard against the mountain on the other side of the fjord that it came back to him again; and when he had thrown it across a few times it became a bridge. They went across the fjord on this bridge, and when they got to the other side the man asked the lad to wind up the yarn again as fast as he could. "For if we do not wind it up quickly the troll women will be upon us and tear us to pieces." The lad wound up the yarn as quickly as he could, and just as he got to the end the troll women came rushing along.

They dashed into the water so that the foam surged round them, and tried to snatch the end; but they could not manage to get hold of it, and so they were drowned in the fjord.

When they had walked on for some days, the companion said:

"We shall soon come to the castle where the princess lives about whom you dreamt, and when we get there you must go in and tell the king your dream, and whom it is you seek."

When they got there the lad did so, and he was well received by the king. He got a room for himself and one for his companion, and when the time for dinner came he was invited to the king's own table. When he saw the princess he recognised her at once, and saw that she was the one about whom he had dreamt, and whom he should have. He told her his errand, and she answered she liked him and would willingly have him, but first he must go through three trials. So when they had dined she gave him a pair of gold scissors, and said:

"The first trial is that you take these and keep them, and give me them back to-morrow at dinner-time. It is not a difficult trial, I should think," she said, with a grin, "but if you cannot do that you will lose your life. That is the law here, and you will be broken on the wheel and your head stuck on a stake, just like the suitors whose skulls you see outside the windows," for there hung human skulls round about the palace, like crows on the fences in the autumn.

"There's not much difficulty in that," thought the lad. But the princess was so merry and boisterous and romped so much with him that he forgot both the scissors and himself; and while they were in the midst of the romping she stole the scissors from him without his knowing it. When he got up to his room in the evening and told his companion what had happened, and what the princess had said about the scissors which she gave him to keep, the companion said:

"Of course, you have the scissors she gave you?"

He felt in all his pockets, but there were no scissors, and the lad became greatly troubled when he found they were gone.

THE TROLL WOMEN DASHED INTO THE WATER, SO THAT THE FOAM SURGED ROUND THEM, AND TRIED TO SNATCH THE END OF THE YARN

"Well, well, you must be patient, and I'll try and get them back for you," said the companion. He then went down to the stable, where there was a big, fat goat which belonged to the princess, and which could fly many times more quickly through the air than it could run over the ground.

Then he took the Three-Sister-Sword, and gave the goat a blow between the horns with it, and said :

"When does the princess ride to her sweetheart to-night?"

The goat bleated and said he dared not tell, but when he got another blow he said the princess would be there at eleven o'clock. The companion put on the Three-Sister-Hat and became invisible, and then waited till she came. The princess took some salve which she had in a big horn, and rubbed the goat with it, and said :

"Through air, through air, over roofs and spires, over land, over water, over hills, over dales, to my sweetheart, who awaits me in the mountain to-night !"

Just as the goat set off the companion jumped up behind, and away they went like the wind through the air. They were not long on the way. All of a sudden they came to a mountain ; there she knocked, and in they rushed to the troll, who was her sweetheart.

"Another suitor has arrived and wants to marry me, my dear. He is young and handsome, but I will have none other than you," she said, making up to the troll. "So I put him on trial, and here are the scissors he was to look after. Now you must take care of them," she said. Then they laughed heartily, as if they already had the lad on wheel and stake.

"Yes, I shall mind them and look after them, and I shall sleep in the arms of my bride when the raven is picking the bones of the lad," said the troll.

Then he placed the scissors in an iron chest with three locks to it ; but just as he dropped the scissors into the chest, the companion took them. No one could see him, for he had on the Three-Sister-Hat ; and the troll thus locked the chest on nothing.

The keys he hid in the hole of one of his back teeth, in which he had the toothache. It would be a difficult job to find them there, he thought.

Soon after midnight the princess set out for the palace again. The companion sat behind her on the goat, and they were not long in getting home.

Next day the lad was asked to dinner at the king's table, but the princess gave herself such mincing airs, and was so stuck up and proud, she would scarcely look at the lad. When they had dined she put on her Sunday expression, and said with a simper :

"I suppose you have the scissors I gave you to keep yesterday?"

"Yes, I have! Here they are!" said the lad, taking them out and banging them on the table, so that it bounded from the floor.

The princess could not have been more angry had he struck her in the face with them; but, notwithstanding this, she made herself pleasant and gentle, and said :

"Since you have looked after the scissors so well, it will not be difficult for you to keep my ball of gold yarn. You can give it me back to-morrow at dinner-time; but if you haven't got it you will lose your life. That is the law here."

"There's not much difficulty about that," thought the lad, and took the ball and put it in his pocket. But she began again to romp and play with him, so that he forgot both himself and the ball; and when they were in the midst of the romping, she stole it from him and let him go.

When he got up to his room and told all they had said and done, the companion said :

"Of course you have the ball she gave you?"

"Yes, that I have," said the lad and felt in his pocket; but no, he had no ball, and he became so troubled again that he did not know what to do with himself.

"Well, be patient! I must try and get it for you," said the companion. He then took the sword and the hat and set off to a smith and got a hundredweight of iron welded on to the sword. When he came to the stable he gave the goat such a blow between the horns that it staggered, and then he asked it when the princess would ride to her sweetheart that night.

"At twelve o'clock," bleated the goat.

The companion put on the Three-Sister-Hat again and waited

THEN THEY LAUGHED HEARTILY, AS IF THEY ALREADY HAD THE LAD ON THE STAKE.

till she came rushing in with the horn and rubbed the goat with the salve. She then said the same as the first time.

"Through air, through air, over roofs and spires, over land, over water, over hills, over dales, to my sweetheart, who awaits me in the mountain to-night."

Just as they set off the companion jumped up behind on the goat and away they went like the wind through the air.

As soon as they came to the troll mountain she knocked

three times and in they rushed to the troll, who was her sweetheart.

"Wherever did you put the scissors I gave you yesterday, my dear?" said the princess; "my suitor had got them back and gave them to me again."

"That can't be possible," said the troll, for he had locked the chest with three locks and hidden the keys in the hole in his back tooth. But when they unlocked the chest they saw the troll had no scissors there. The princess then told him she had given the suitor her ball of gold yarn.

"Here it is," she said, "for I took it from him again without his knowing it. But what had we better think of since he can do such tricks?"

The troll did not quite know, but when they had thought it over a bit they decided to make a big fire and burn the ball; they would then be sure he would not get it. Just as she threw the ball into the fire the companion stood ready and caught it. Neither of them saw it, for he had the Three-Sister-Hat on. When the princess had been with the troll awhile and the day began to dawn she set off to the palace again; the companion sat behind her on the goat and they got home both quickly and well.

When the lad was asked to dinner the companion gave him the ball. The princess was still more stuck up and proud than on the day before, and when they had finished she pouted and said:

"I suppose I may have back my ball which I gave you to keep yesterday?"

"Yes," said the lad, "that you may. Here it is!" and he threw it down with such force that the table gave a jump and the king leapt into the air.

The princess turned as white as a ghost, but she soon recovered herself and said that was well done; and now there was only one little trial left.

"If you are so clever that you can bring me to-morrow at dinner-time what I am now thinking about you shall have me and keep me," she said.

The lad felt as if he had been condemned to death, for he thought it was impossible to know what she was thinking about and still more impossible to get it. When he came to his room he was so excited he could not keep still. The companion said if he would be quiet he would find a way out of the difficulty as he had done before, and at last the lad was pacified and lay down to sleep.

In the meantime the companion rushed off to the smith and had two hundredweight of iron welded to the sword; when that was done he went to the stable and struck the goat between the horns with it so that it staggered from wall to wall.

"When is the princess going to her sweetheart to-night?" said he.

"At one o'clock," bleated the goat.

When the time came the companion stood in the stable with the Three-Sister-Hat on, and when the princess had rubbed the goat with the salve and uttered the same words as before that they should fly to her sweetheart, who was waiting for her in the mountain, she set off through the air and wind with the companion again behind her. But this time he was not so gentle with the princess, for every now and then he thumped her so that he almost maimed her. When they came to the mountain she knocked at the gate, which opened and they rushed in to her sweetheart.

When she got there she began to moan and groan and said she did not know if the weather could have been so bad, but both she and the goat had been beaten by some one and she was sure she must be black and blue all over, so badly had she fared on the way. She then told him how her suitor had given her back the ball also, but neither she nor the troll could make out how it had happened.

"But do you know what I have thought of now?" she said.

No, that the troll could not tell.

"Well, I have told him to bring me by dinner-time to-morrow that which I was thinking of—and that was your head! Do you think he can get that, my dear?" said the princess, and began fondling the troll.

"I don't think he can," said the troll; that he would take his oath on; so he laughed and roared worse than a bogie; and both the troll and the princess thought the lad was more likely to adorn the wheel and stake, with the ravens to peck his eyes out, than to get hold of the troll's head.

When it got towards morning she began to get ready to set out for the palace; but she was afraid, she said. She thought there was some one after her and she dared not go home alone; the troll must go with her. Yes, he would, so he brought out his goat, for he had one just like the princess's and he rubbed it well between the horns with the salve. When he had seated himself the companion got up behind him and off they went through the air to the palace; but on the way the companion struck the troll and the goat time after time, and gave them blow after blow with his sword, till at last they sank lower and lower and at last they nearly sank into the ocean across which they were passing. When the troll saw that things were going so badly he hastened on to the palace with the princess, but stopped to see that she got in well and safely. But just as she shut the door behind her the companion cut off the troll's head and ran up to the lad's room with it.

"Here is that which the princess thought of," said he.

The lad was, as you can imagine, in high spirits, and when he was asked down to dinner next day and they had finished eating, the princess became as blithe as a lark.

"I suppose you have that which I thought of," said she.

"Indeed, I have," said the lad, and pulled out the head from under the tail of his coat and struck the table with it, so that the table and everything on it fell over.

The princess became as pale as a corpse, but she could not deny that that was what she had thought of, and now he might have her for his wife as she had promised.

The wedding was then kept and there was great rejoicing over the whole kingdom. The companion took the lad aside and told him that he must shut his eyes and pretend to sleep on the wedding night, but if he valued his life, and would obey him, he must not have a wink of sleep before he had rid the princess of the troll-skin, with which she was covered. He would have to flog it off her with a rod made of nine new birch besoms and strip her of it in three tubs of milk. First he was to scrub her in a tub of last year's whey, then he was to rub her in sour milk, and then rinse her in a tub of new milk. The besoms lay under the bed, and the tubs he had placed in the corner, so everything was ready for him.

Yes, the lad promised that he would obey him, and do what he had said. When they went to bed in the evening the lad pretended to sleep. The princess raised herself on her elbow and tickled him under the nose to see if he slept, but the lad seemed to sleep soundly. She then pulled him by his hair and beard, but he slept like a log, as she thought. Then she dragged out from under her pillow a large butcher's knife, and was going to cut his head off, when the lad sprang up, struck the knife out of her hand, and seized hold of her by the hair. He flogged her with the birch rods till they were worn out and there was not a twig left of them. When this was done, he threw her into the tub of whey, and then he saw what sort of a creature she was. She was as black as a raven all over her body, but when he had scrubbed her in the whey and rubbed her with the sour milk, and rinsed her in the new milk, the troll-skin was gone and she was as gentle and beautiful as she had never been before.

The next day the companion said they must set off home. The lad was quite willing and the princess also, for her dowry had been ready a long time. During the night the companion had brought all the gold and silver and valuables, which had belonged to the troll in the mountain, to the palace; and when they were ready to set out the next day, they found the courtyard so full of things they could hardly move. That dowry was worth more than the king's realm, and they could not tell how they were to take it with them. But the companion knew a way out of every difficulty; there were six goats belonging to the troll, which could all fly through the air; and these they loaded so heavily with gold and silver, that they had to walk along the ground, as they were unable to rise in the air and fly, and what the goats could not carry they had to leave behind at the palace.

So they travelled far, and further than far, till the goats at last became so tired and worn out that they were unable to go any further. The lad and the princess did not know what to do, but when the companion saw they could not get on, he took the whole dowry on his back and the goats on the top, and carried them all till there was only a mile left to the lad's home. Then the companion said, "Now I must leave you, I cannot remain with you any longer." But the lad would not part with him; he would not lose him for little or much. So he went with them another half mile, but further he could not go, and when the lad begged and prayed him to stop with him, or at least be present at the homecoming at his father's, the companion said no, that he could not. The lad then asked him what he owed him for all his help and assistance. If it was to be anything, it must be the half of everything he got during the next five years, said the companion.

Yes, that he should have.

When he was gone the lad left all his riches behind him and went home empty handed.

They then had such a home-coming festival, that it was heard and spoken of over seven kingdoms, and when it was at an end, the winter had set in; and then they began to cart home all the gold and silver, both with the goats and the twelve horses which his father had.

In five years the companion came back for his share. The man had then everything divided into two equal parts.

"But there is one thing which you have not divided," said the companion.

"What is that?" said the man. "I thought I had divided everything."

"You have a child," said the companion; "you must divide that also in two."

"NOW THEY MUST PART FOR EVER," SAID THE COMPANION

Yes, that was true enough. So he took the sword; but just as he lifted it to cleave the child in two, the companion seized the point of the sword from behind, so that he could not strike.

"Are you not glad that I stopped you from striking that blow?" he said.

"Yes, I have never been so glad," said the man.

"Well, I was just as glad when you lifted me out of the block of ice. Keep everything you have! I do not want anything, for I am a floating spirit." He was the vintner who had stood in the block of ice outside the church door, and whom all had spat upon; and he had been his companion and helped him because he had given all he had to provide him peace and get him buried in Christian soil. He had been allowed to follow him for a year, and that was over when they parted the last time. But he had been allowed to see him again, and now they must part for ever, for he heard the bells of heaven ringing for him.

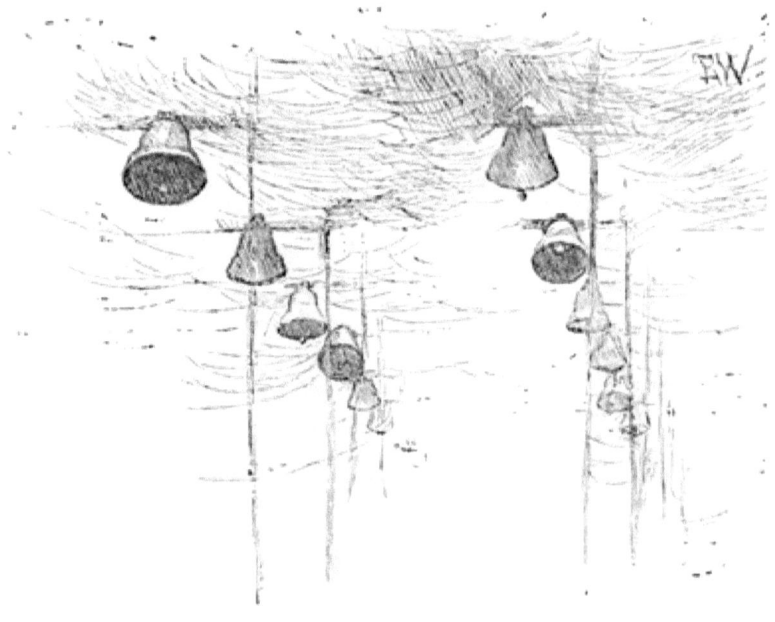

NANNY WHO WOULDN'T GO HOME TO SUPPER

There was once upon a time a woman who had a son and a goat. The son was called Espen and the goat they called Nanny. But they were not good friends, and did not get on together, for the goat was perverse and wayward, as goats will be, and she would never go home at the right time for her supper. So it happened one evening that Espen went out to fetch her home, and when he had been looking for her a while he saw Nanny high, high up on a crag:

"My dear Nanny, you must not stay any longer up there; you must come home now, it is just supper time. I am so hungry and want my supper."

"No, I shan't," said Nanny, "not before I have finished the grass on this tussock, and that tussock—and this and that tussock."

"Then I'll go and tell mother," said the lad.

"That you may, and then I shall be left to eat in peace," said Nanny.

So Espen went and told his mother.

"Go to the fox and ask him to bite Nanny," said his mother.

The lad went to the fox. "My dear fox, bite Nanny, for Nanny won't come home in time. I am so hungry, and I want my supper," said Espen.

"No, I don't want to spoil my snout on pig's bristles and goat's beard," said the fox.

So the lad went and told his mother.

"Well, go to the wolf," said his mother.

The lad went to the wolf: "My dear wolf, tear the fox, for the fox won't bite Nanny, and Nanny won't come home in time. I am so hungry, and I want my supper."

"No," said the wolf, "I won't wear out my paws and teeth on a skinny fox."

So the lad went and told his mother.

"Well, go to the bear and ask him to slay the wolf," said the mother.

The lad went to the bear. "My dear bear, slay the wolf, for the wolf won't tear the fox, and the fox won't bite Nanny, and Nanny won't come home in time. I am so hungry and want my supper."

"No, that I won't," said the bear; "I don't want to wear out my claws for that."

So the lad went and told his mother.

"Well, go to the Finn and ask him to shoot the bear."

The lad went to the Finn. "My dear Finn, shoot the bear, for the bear won't slay the wolf, the wolf won't tear the fox, the fox won't bite Nanny, and Nanny won't come home in time. I am so hungry and want my supper."

"No, I will not," said the Finn; "I am not going to shoot away my bullets for that."

So the lad went and told his mother.

"Well go to the fir," said his mother, "and ask it to crush the Finn."

The lad went to the fir-tree: "My dear fir, crush the Finn, for the Finn won't shoot the bear, the bear won't slay the wolf, the wolf won't tear the fox, the fox won't bite Nanny, and Nanny won't come home in time. I am so hungry and want my supper."

"No, I will not," said the fir, "I am not going to break my boughs for that."

So the lad went and told his mother.

"Well, go to the fire," said his mother, "and ask it to burn the fir."

The lad went to the fire: "My dear fire, burn the fir, for the fir won't crush the Finn, the Finn won't shoot the bear, the bear won't slay the wolf, the wolf won't tear the fox, the fox won't bite Nanny, and Nanny won't come home in time. I am so hungry and want my supper."

"No, I will not," said the fire, "I am not going to burn myself out for that."

So the lad went and told his mother.

"Well, go to the water, and ask it to quench the fire," she said.

The lad went to the water. "My dear water, quench the fire, for the fire won't burn the fir, the fir won't crush the Finn, the Finn won't shoot the bear, the bear won't slay the wolf, the wolf won't tear the fox, the fox won't bite Nanny, and Nanny won't come home in time. I am so hungry and want my supper."

"No, I will not," said the water, "I am not going to waste myself for that."

So the lad went and told his mother.

"Well, go to the ox," said she, "and ask him to drink up the water."

The lad went to the ox : "My dear ox, drink up the water, for the water won't quench the fire, the fire won't burn the fir, the fir won't crush the Finn, the Finn won't shoot the bear, the bear won't slay the wolf, the wolf won't tear the fox, the fox won't bite Nanny, and Nanny won't come home in time. I am so hungry and want my supper."

"No, I will not," said the ox. "I'm not going to burst myself for that."

So the lad went and told his mother.

"Well, go to the yoke," said she, "and ask it to throttle the ox."

The lad went to the yoke. "My dear yoke, throttle the ox, for the ox won't drink the water, the water won't quench the fire, the fire won't burn the fir, the fir won't crush the Finn, the Finn won't shoot the bear, the bear won't slay the wolf, the wolf won't tear the fox, the fox won't bite Nanny, and Nanny won't come home in time. I am so hungry and want my supper."

"No, I will not," said the yoke. "I'm not going to break myself in two for that."

So the lad went and told his mother.

"Well, go to the axe," said she, "and tell it to split the yoke."

The lad went to the axe. "My dear axe, split the yoke, for the yoke won't throttle the ox, the ox won't drink the water, the water won't quench the fire, the fire won't burn the fir, the fir won't crush the Finn, the Finn won't shoot the bear, the bear won't slay the wolf, the wolf won't tear the fox, the fox won't bite Nanny, and Nanny won't come home in time. I am so hungry and want my supper."

"No, I will not," said the axe. "I am not going to blunt my edge for that."

So the lad went and told his mother.

"Well, go to the smith," said she, "and ask him to hammer the axe."

The lad went to the smith. "My dear smith! hammer the

axe, for the axe won't split the yoke, the yoke won't throttle the ox, the ox won't drink the water, the water won't quench the fire, the fire won't burn the fir, the fir won't crush the Finn, the Finn won't shoot the bear, the bear won't slay the wolf, the wolf won't tear the fox, the fox won't bite Nanny, and Nanny won't come home in time. I am so hungry and want my supper."

"No, I will not," said the smith. "I'll not burn my coals and wear out my sledge-hammers for that."

So the lad went and told his mother.

"Well, go to the rope," said she, "and ask it to hang the smith."

The lad went to the rope. "My dear rope, hang the smith, for the smith won't hammer the axe, the axe won't split the yoke, the yoke won't throttle the ox, the ox won't drink the water, the water won't quench the fire, the fire won't burn the fir, the fir won't crush the Finn, the Finn won't shoot the bear, the bear won't slay the wolf, the wolf won't tear the fox, the fox won't bite Nanny, and Nanny won't come home in time. I am so hungry and want my supper."

"No, I will not," said the rope. "I'm not going to break in two for that."

So the lad went and told his mother.

"Well, go to the mouse," said she, "and ask her to gnaw the rope."

The lad went to the mouse. "My dear mouse, gnaw the rope, for the rope won't hang the smith, the smith won't hammer the axe, the axe won't split the yoke, the yoke won't throttle the ox, the ox won't drink the water, the water won't quench the fire, the fire won't burn the fir, the fir won't crush the Finn, the Finn won't shoot the bear, the bear won't slay the wolf, the wolf won't tear the fox, the fox won't bite Nanny, and Nanny won't come home in time. I am so hungry and want my supper."

"No, I will not," said the mouse. "I'm not going to wear out my teeth for that."

So the lad went and told his mother.

"Well, go to the cat," said she, "and ask her to catch the mouse."

The lad went to the cat. "My dear cat, catch the mouse, for the mouse won't gnaw the rope, the rope won't hang the smith, the smith won't hammer the axe, the axe won't split the yoke, the

yoke won't throttle the ox, the ox won't drink the water, the water won't quench the fire, the fire won't burn the fir, the fir won't crush the Finn, the Finn won't shoot the bear, the bear won't slay the wolf, the wolf won't tear the fox, the fox won't bite Nanny, and Nanny won't come home in time. I am so hungry and want my supper."

"Yes, but give me a drop of milk for my kittens, and then——" said the cat.

Yes, that she should have. So the cat caught the mouse, and the mouse gnawed the rope, and the rope hanged the smith, and the smith hammered the axe, and the axe split the yoke, and the yoke throttled the ox, and the ox drank the water, and the water quenched the fire, and the fire burned the fir, and the fir crushed the Finn, and the Finn shot the bear, and the bear slew the wolf, and the wolf tore the fox, and the fox bit Nanny, and Nanny took to her heels, scampered home, and ran against the barn wall and broke one of her legs.

"M—a—h—a—h!" bleated the goat. There she lay, and if she isn't dead she is still limping about on three legs. But Espen said it served her right, because she would not come home in time for supper that day.

THE LAD WITH THE BEER KEG

ONCE upon a time there was a lad who had served a long time with a man north of Dovrefjeld. This man was a master at brewing beer, and it was so wonderfully good that the like of it was not to be found anywhere. When the lad was going to leave and the man was to pay him the wages he had earned he would not have anything but a keg of the Christmas beer. That he got and off he went with it, and he carried it both far and long. But the longer he carried the keg the heavier it got, and so he began to look round to see if any one were coming with whom he could drink, so that the beer might get less and the keg lighter.

After a long time he met an old man with a long beard.

"Good day!" said the man.

"Good day!" said the lad.

"Where are you going?" said the man.

"I'm looking for some one to drink with me, so that I can get my keg lightened," said the lad.

"Can't you drink with me just as well as with any one else?" said the man. "I have travelled far and wide, so I am both tired and thirsty."

"Well, why not?" said the lad. "But where do you come from, and who are you?" said he.

"I am the Lord and I come from heaven," said the man.

"I will not drink with you," said the lad, "for you make such a difference between people in this world, and divide everything so unjustly, that some become rich and some poor. No, I will not drink with you," said he, and trudged off again with his keg.

When he had gone a bit on the way the keg again became so heavy that he could not carry it any longer unless some one came to drink with him and lessen the beer in the keg. He then met an ugly, bony man, who came rushing along.

"Good day!" said the man.

"Good day!" said the lad.

"Where are you going?" said the man.

"Oh, I'm looking for some one to drink with me, so that I can lighten my keg," said the boy.

"Can't you drink just as well with me as with any one else?" said the man. "I have travelled far and wide and a drop of beer will do an old body good," said he.

"Yes, why not?" said the lad; "but who are you and where do you come from?" he asked.

"I? Oh, I am well known. I am the Devil, and I come from hell," said the man.

"No," said the lad, "you only torture and plague people, and whenever there is a misfortune they always say it is your fault. No, I will not drink with you," said the lad. So he went far and further than far with his beer keg, till he felt it growing so heavy he could not carry it any further. He began to look round again if some one were not coming with whom he could drink and so lighten his keg.

After a long time there came a man who was so thin and shrivelled it was a wonder his bones could hang together.

"Good day!" said the man.

"Good day!" said the lad.

"Where are you going?" said the man.

"I'm looking to see if I can find some one to drink with me," said the lad, "so as to lighten my keg a little; it is getting so heavy to carry," said he.

"Can't you just as well drink with me as with any one else?" said the man.

"Yes; why not?" said the lad; "but who are you?"

"They call me Death," said the man.

"I will drink with you," said the lad, and he put down the

"THEY CALL ME DEATH," SAID THE MAN

keg and began to pour out the beer into a bowl. "You are a trustworthy man, for you treat all alike, both rich and poor."

So he drank his health, and Death thought it was a splendid drink; and as the lad did not begrudge him, they drank in turn, so the beer got less and the keg lighter. At last Death said:

"I have never known drink which tasted better and did me so much good as the beer you have given me. I feel as if I had been born anew. I don't know what good I can do you in return." When he had bethought himself a while he said that the keg should never get empty, no matter how much they drank of it; and the beer that was in it should become a healing draught, so that the lad should cure the sick better than any doctor. Death also said that when the lad came into a sick room he would always be there and show himself to him, and it should be a sure sign to him that when Death sat at the foot of the bed he would be able to cure the sick with a draught from the keg, but if he sat at the head there was no help or cure for the sick person.

The lad soon became renowned, and was sent for far and wide, and he helped many to health again for whom there had been no hope.

When he came into a room and saw Death beside the sick he foretold either life or death, and he was always right in his prediction. He became a rich and mighty man, and one day he was fetched to a princess far away in another land. She was so dangerously ill that the doctors thought they could do no more for her, so they promised him anything he might wish for if he only saved her life.

When he came into the princess's room he found Death sitting at the head of the bed, but he sat dozing and nodding, and while he sat thus the princess felt better.

"This is a case of life or death," said the doctor, "and there is no hope, if I see rightly," he said; but they told him he must save her if it should cost even the whole kingdom. He then looked at Death, and while he was sitting dozing he made a sign to the servants that they should make haste and turn the bed. So Death was left sitting at the foot of it, and as soon as that was done he gave the princess the healing draught, and she was saved.

"Now you've cheated me," said Death, "and we are quits."

"I was obliged to do it if I were to win the kingdom," said the doctor.

"That will not help you much," said Death; "your time is up, and now you belong to me."

"Let that be as it may," said the doctor; "but I suppose

"NOW YOU'VE CHEATED ME," SAID DEATH

you'll first give me leave to read the Lord's Prayer to the end," said he.

Yes, that he would; but the doctor took great care not to read the Lord's Prayer. He read everything else, but the Lord's

Prayer never crossed his lips. At last he thought he had cheated Death for good; but when Death thought this had gone on too long, he went to the doctor's room one night and hung up a large tablet opposite his bed with the Lord's Prayer on it.

When the doctor awoke he began reading it, and did not bethink himself of what he was doing till he came to "Amen." But then it was too late.

LITTLE FRED AND HIS FIDDLE

ONCE upon a time there was a cottager who had an only son, and this lad was rather weak and always ailing, so he was not able to go out to work. His name was Fred, but being rather small for his age he was generally called Little Fred. At home there wasn't much to bite or to munch either, so his father went about the parish to get a place for him as a cow-boy or an errand-boy.

But nobody wanted a lad until he came to the bailiff of the parish; he would take him as he had just turned away his errand-boy, and there was no one who cared to go to him, because every one said he was a stingy old miser. "Something is better than nothing," thought the father; in any case he would get his food, for that was all he was going to have from the bailiff. There wasn't a word said about clothes or wages.

But when the lad had been there three years he wanted to leave, and so the bailiff paid him his wages for the time he had been with him. He was to have a penny a year. "It couldn't very well be less," said the bailiff, so he paid the lad three pennies altogether. Little Fred, however, thought it was a lot of money, because he had never owned so much before; but he asked if he wasn't going to have some more, for all that.

"You have got more than you ought to have," said the bailiff.

"Shan't I have anything for clothes, then?" said Little Fred. "Those I had on when I came here are now all in rags, and I haven't had any new ones from you. I have only rags and tatters flapping and dangling about me," said he.

"When you have got what we agreed upon, and the three pennies besides, I have nothing more to do with you," said the bailiff. But he might go out into the kitchen and get a little food in his knapsack, and then he started off along the road to town to buy clothes. He was both merry and glad, because he had never seen a penny before, and he couldn't help feeling in his pocket now and then to see if they were all three there.

So when he had gone far, and further than far, he came to a narrow valley with high mountains on all sides; so he didn't know which way to get on, and he began to wonder what there could be on the other side of the mountains and how he should get over them. But get over them he must, and so he started. He wasn't very strong, and had to rest now and then, and he would then count over his money to see how much he had.

When he got to the top of the mountain he found there was nothing but a great big moor. There he sat down, and was just going to see if he had his pennies all right when a beggar came up to him before he knew a thing about it; but the beggar was so tall and big that the lad began to scream when he really saw what a big and long fellow he was.

"Don't you be afraid of me," said the beggar; "I shan't hurt you. I only beg for a penny in heaven's name."

"God help me," said the lad; "I have only three pennies, and I was just going to town to buy some clothes with them."

"It is worse with me than with you," said the beggar; "I haven't got a penny, and I am still more ragged than you."

"Well, I suppose you must have it, then," said the lad.

When he had walked on a bit he became tired and sat down to take another rest. When he looked up there was a beggar

"DON'T YOU BE AFRAID OF ME," SAID THE BEGGAR

again, but this one was much bigger and uglier than the first, and when the lad saw how big and ugly he was he began to scream.

"Don't be afraid of me; I shan't hurt you. I only beg for a penny in heaven's name," said the beggar.

"Well, God help me!" said the lad, "as true as I am here, I have only got two pennies, and I was just going to town to buy some clothes with them. If only I had met you sooner, I——"

"It is worse with me than with you," said the beggar. "I haven't got a penny, and I have a much bigger body and less clothes."

"Well, I suppose you must have it then!" said the lad.

When he got a bit further he became tired, and sat down to rest; but he had no sooner sat down than another beggar came to him; and he was so tall and big and ugly, that when the lad was going to look up at him he had to look up to the sky, and then he could really see what a very big, ugly, ragged fellow he was. And the lad began screaming and shouting.

"Don't you be afraid of me, my lad;" said the beggar; "I shan't hurt you, for I am only a poor beggar, who begs a penny in heaven's name."

"Well, God help me!" said the lad, "as true as I am here, I have only one penny left, and I was just going to town to buy some clothes with it. If I had only met you sooner, I——"

"Well, I haven't got a penny and I have a bigger body and less clothes, so it is worse with me than with you," said the beggar.

"Well, I suppose you must have the penny, then," said Little Fred. There was no help for it; now they had all had one each and he had none.

"Now since you have such a good heart, and have given away all you had," said the beggar, "I will give you a wish for each penny." It was the same beggar who had got all the three pennies; he had only changed each time, so that the lad should not know him again.

"I have always been wishing to hear the fiddle playing, and see people so merry and happy that they had to dance," said the lad;

"so if I may wish what I like I wish I had such a fiddle as would make everything that is alive dance to its tune."

"That you may have," said the beggar; "but it is a poor wish. You must wish something better for the other pennies."

"I have always been fond of hunting and shooting," said Little Fred; "so if I may wish what I like, I wish I had a gun that would hit everything I aim at, if it were ever so far off."

"That you may have," said the beggar; "but it is a poor wish. You must wish something better for the last penny."

"I have always liked to be in company with kind and good people," said Little Fred; "so if I may wish what I like, I wish that no one can refuse me the first thing I ask."

"That wasn't such a bad wish," said the beggar, and strolled off among the hills till the lad couldn't see him any more. So the lad lay down to sleep, and the next day he came down from the mountains with his fiddle and his gun.

First he went to the storekeeper and asked for clothes, and at one farm he asked for a horse, and at another for a sledge, and at one place he asked for a fur coat, and no one could say "No" to him; even the most stingy people had to give him what he asked for. At last he travelled through the parish like a fine gentleman with his horse and sledge. When he had gone some distance he met the bailiff he had served.

"Good-day, master!" said Little Fred, as he stopped and took off his cap.

"Good-day!" said the bailiff; "have I been your master?"

"Yes, don't you recollect that I served three years with you for three pennies?" said Little Fred.

"Dear me!" said the bailiff, "how you have got on! How is it you have become such a grand fellow?"

"Ah, you think so, do you?" said the youngster.

"And you seem to be so merry that you must have a fiddle with you as well," said the bailiff.

"Yes, I always liked to see people dance," said the lad, "but the finest thing I have is this gun of mine. It hits everything I aim at, if it is ever so far off. Do you see that magpie in the fir-tree yonder? What will you wager I don't hit it from where we are now standing?"

The bailiff would willingly have staked both his horse and farm and a hundred dollars besides, that he couldn't hit it. But as it was he would stake all the money he had in his pocket, and wouldn't mind fetching the magpie when it fell down, because he never believed it was possible a gun could reach so far. Off went the gun and down fell the magpie right in the middle of a lot of brambles. The bailiff ran right in among the brambles after the magpie, picked it up and showed it to the lad. But just at that moment Little Fred took his fiddle out and began playing, and the bailiff began to dance, and danced away while the thorns were tearing his clothes; but the lad went on playing and the bailiff danced and cried and begged for himself till the rags flew about him and till he had scarcely a thread to his back.

"Well now, I think you are almost as ragged as I was when I left your service," said the lad, "so now you may go." But first the bailiff had to pay the wager he had lost, that the boy couldn't hit the magpie.

When the lad came to town, he went into an inn, and began playing, and all who came there had to dance. And he lived on merrily and well, for he had no cares, since no one could say "No" to him when he asked for anything.

But just as they were in the middle of the fun the watchman came to take the lad up before the magistrate, for the bailiff had complained about him and charged him with having waylaid and robbed him and nearly taken his life; and now the lad was going to be hanged—there was no help for it.

But Little Fred had the means of getting out of all trouble, and that was the fiddle. He began to play on it, and then you should have seen how the watchmen danced away, till they fell down and gasped for breath.

So they sent soldiers and the guard, but it fared no better with them than the watchmen. When Little Fred took out his fiddle, they had to dance as long as he was able to play on it, but they were done for long before he was tired. At last they came unawares upon him and took him while he was asleep at night, and when he was brought up he was sentenced to be hanged at once, and away they all went to the gallows. There was such a crowd of people to see this wonderful lad, and the bailiff was there too; he was so pleased, because he was to get amends both for his money and his skin and see the lad hanged into the bargain; but it took a long time before they came to the gallows, because Little Fred was always weak on his legs, and now he made himself still worse. He had brought with him his fiddle and his gun, as they could not get him to part with them, and when he came to the gallows and was going to mount the ladder, he halted and rested himself on each step. When he got to the top of the ladder he sat down and asked, if they would not grant him one thing; he had such a wish to play a tune—just a little bit of a tune—on his fiddle before he was hanged. "Well," they said, "it were both sin and shame to deny him that;" for you see they could not say "No" to what he asked for. But the bailiff asked in heaven's name that they would not let him touch a string, or else there would not be much left of any of them. If the lad was to play the bailiff wanted to be tied up to a birch tree that stood there. But Little Fred was not long about getting out his fiddle and playing on it, and then all that were there began dancing, both those that went on two legs and those that went on four, both the deacon and the parson, the judge and the sheriff, men and women, dogs and swine; they danced and screamed the one louder than the other. Some danced till they dropped down dead, some danced till they fell down in fits. All had a terrible time of it, but worst of all the poor bailiff who was tied up to the birch-tree, and was dancing away till he scraped great bits of skin off his back. There was no one who thought of doing anything to Little Fred after that, and they let him go with his gun and his fiddle where he liked. He lived happy all his days, for there was no one who could say "No" to the first thing he asked for.

EVERY ONE THAT WAS THERE BEGAN DANCING; THEY DANCED AND SCREAMED THE ONE LOUDER THAN THE OTHER

THE STOREHOUSE KEY IN THE DISTAFF

There was once a rich farmer's son who went out to woo. He had heard of a lass who was fair and gentle, and who was both clever in the house and good at cooking.

Thither he went, for it was just such a wife he wanted. The people on the farm knew, of course, on what errand he came, so they asked him to take a seat near to them, and they talked and chatted with him, as the custom is, and besides offered him a drink and asked him to stop to dinner. They went in and out of the room, so the lad had time to look about him, and over in a corner he saw a spinning wheel with the distaff full of flax.

"Whose spinning wheel is that?" asked the lad.

"Oh, that's our daughter's," said the woman of the house.

"There's a deal of flax on it," said the lad; "I suppose she takes more than a day to spin that," said he.

"No, not at all," said the woman; "she does it easily in one day and perhaps less than that."

That was more than he had ever heard of any one being able to spin in such a short time.

When they were going to carry in the dinner they all went out of the room, and he was left alone. He then saw an old key lying in the window, and this he took and stowed well away among the flax on the distaff. So they ate and drank and got on well together, and when the lad thought he had been there long enough, he said good-bye, and went his way. They asked him to come soon again, which he promised, but he did not speak of the matter he had at heart, although he liked the lass very well.

Some time after he came again to the farm, and they received him still better than the first time. But just as they were chatting at their best, the farmer's wife said:

"Last time you were here something very remarkable happened; our storehouse key disappeared all at once, and we have never been able to find it since."

The lad went over to the spinning wheel, which stood in the corner with just as much flax on it as when last he was there. He put his hand in among the flax, and said:

"Here is the key! much cannot be made by the spinning, when the spinning day lasts from Michaelmas to Easter!"

So he said good-bye, and did not speak of the matter he had at heart that time either.

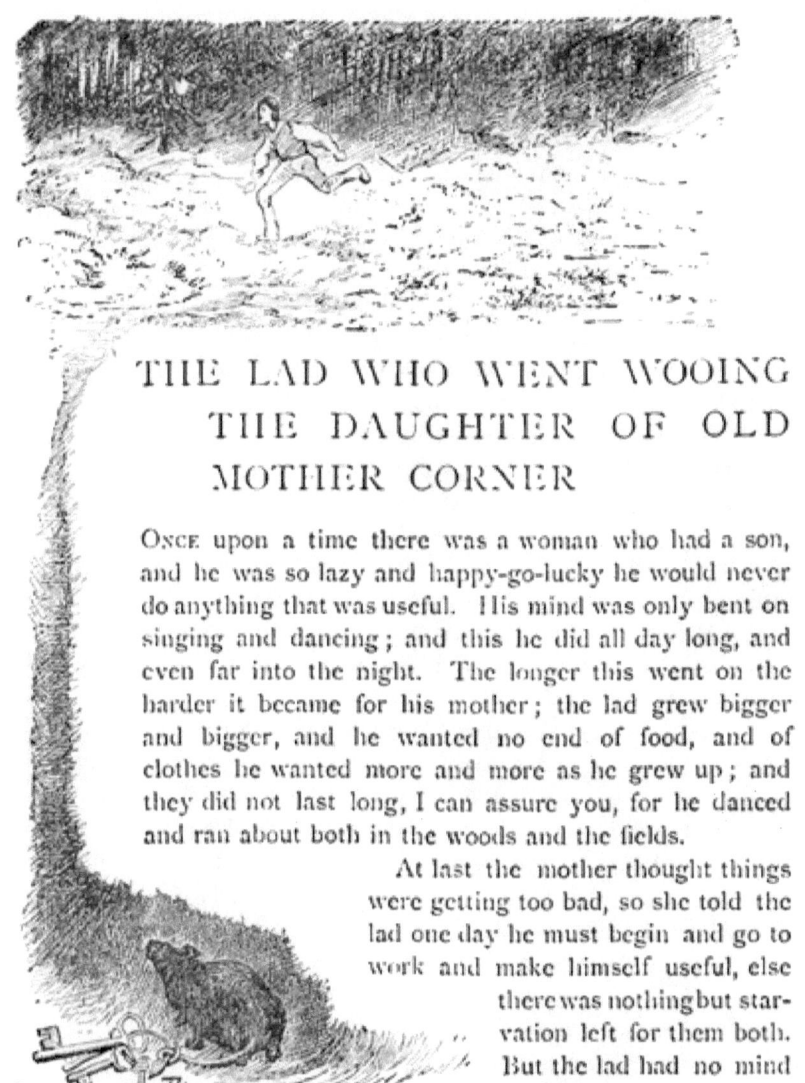

THE LAD WHO WENT WOOING THE DAUGHTER OF OLD MOTHER CORNER

ONCE upon a time there was a woman who had a son, and he was so lazy and happy-go-lucky he would never do anything that was useful. His mind was only bent on singing and dancing; and this he did all day long, and even far into the night. The longer this went on the harder it became for his mother; the lad grew bigger and bigger, and he wanted no end of food, and of clothes he wanted more and more as he grew up; and they did not last long, I can assure you, for he danced and ran about both in the woods and the fields.

At last the mother thought things were getting too bad, so she told the lad one day he must begin and go to work and make himself useful, else there was nothing but starvation left for them both. But the lad had no mind for that; he said he would rather go and woo the daughter of old Mother Corner, for if he got her he could live happy and contented all his days, and sing and dance, and never trouble himself about work. When the mother heard this she thought that was not a bad thing after all; he might try in any case, and so she dressed up the lad as best she could, that he might look a little tidy when he came to old Mother Corner, and then he set out on his way.

When he came out of the house the sun was shining warm and bright; but it had rained during the night, so the ground was soft, and the moors were filled with puddles. The lad took the shortest way across the moors to old Mother Corner, and ran and sang as he always did, but just as he was running and jumping along he came to a bridge of logs, across a marshy bit of the path, and from this bridge he was going to make a jump across a puddle on to a tussock, so as not to dirty his boots, but just as he put his foot on the tussock—plump! down he went and did not stop till he found himself in a nasty, dark hole. At first he could not see anything, but when he had been there awhile he caught a glimpse of a rat, widdling-waddling about with a bunch of keys on her tail.

"Are you there, my dear?" said the rat. "I am so glad you have come to see me. I have been waiting a long time for you. I expect you have come to woo me, and that you are in a great hurry; but you must be patient awhile yet, for I must have a big dowry, and I am not ready for the wedding, but I'll do my best so that it can come off soon."

When she had said this, she brought out some egg-shells with all kinds of dainties, such as rats eat, and put before him, and said: "You must make yourself at home and have something to eat; you must be both tired and hungry."

But the lad did not much fancy such food. "I wish I were well out of this and above ground again," he thought; but he said nothing.

"I suppose you want to be off home," said the rat. "I know you are longing for the wedding, so I'll make all the haste I can.

You must take with you this linen thread, and when you get up above ground you must not look back, but go straight home; and on the road you must not say anything but 'Short in front and long behind,'" and so she put into his hand a linen thread.

"Heaven be praised!" said the lad when he got above ground; "I shall never go down there again." But he had the thread in his hand, and he ran and sang as usual. But although he did not think any more about the rat-hole, the tune had got into his head, and he sang:

"Short in front and long behind!
Short in front and long behind!"

When he got home to the door he turned round, and there lay many, many hundreds of yards of the whitest linen, so fine that the cleverest weavers could not weave it finer.

"Mother, mother! come out, come out!" he shouted and cried.

The woman came running out and asked what was the matter. When she saw the linen, which reached as far as she could see and a bit farther, she would not believe her own eyes until the lad had told her how it had happened; and when she had heard it all and felt the linen with her fingers she became so glad that she too began to dance and sing.

She then took the linen and cut it up, and made shirts both for the son and herself. The rest she went to the town with and sold, and got money for. Now they both lived happy and comfortable for awhile. But when it all came to an end the woman had no more food in the house, and so she said to her son that now he must really begin and go to work and make himself useful, else there was nothing left but starvation for both of them.

But the lad had a greater mind to go to old Mother Corner's and woo her daughter. Well, the woman thought that was a good thing, for he was now better dressed and did not look so bad after all. So she dressed and tidied him the best she could, and he brought out his new shoes and polished them until they were so bright that he could see himself in them. After that he set out, and it all happened as before.

When he came outside the sun shone so warm and bright, but it had rained during the night and the ground was soft and muddy, and the moors were filled with puddles.

The lad took the shortest way across the moors to old Mother Corner, and ran and sang as he always did. He went by a different path this time; but just as he was running and jumping along he came to the bridge of logs across the marshy bit of the path, and from this bridge he was going to jump across a puddle on to a tussock, so as not to dirty his boots. But just as he put his foot on the tussock—plump! down he went, and did not stop till he found himself in a nasty, dark hole. At first he saw nothing, but when he had been there awhile he caught sight of a rat, who widdled-waddled about with a bunch of keys on her tail.

"Are you there, my dear?" said the rat. "Welcome again! It was kind of you to come and see me so soon. I know you are quite impatient, but you must really wait awhile; for there is something still wanting for my dowry. But when you come again next time everything shall be ready."

When she had said this, she brought out many kinds of dainty bits in egg-shells, such as rats like to eat; but the lad thought they looked like leavings, and he said he had no appetite. "I only wish I were well out of this," he thought, but he said nothing.

After a while the rat said:

"I suppose you want to be off home again! I'll hurry on with the wedding as quickly as I can, but this time you must take this woollen yarn with you, and when you get above ground you must not look back, but go straight home; and on the way you must not say anything but 'Short in front and long behind.'" And then she gave the woollen yarn into his hand.

"Heaven be praised that I am out of it!" said the lad to himself; "I shall never go there again." And so he sang and leapt as usual. He did not think any more about the rat-hole, but the tune had got into his head, and he went on singing:

> "Short in front and long behind!
> Short in front and long behind!"

And this he kept up all the way home. When he got outside the door he happened to look round, and there lay the finest cloth, many hundreds of yards long, nearly a mile in all, and so fine that the smartest man in town did not have finer cloth in his coat.

"Mother, mother! come out, come out!" cried the lad.

The woman came to the door, held up her hands in astonishment, and nearly fainted with joy when she saw all the beautiful cloth. He then had to tell her how he had got it, and how it had happened from first to last.

They were then well off, as you may imagine. The boy got fine new clothes and the woman went to town and sold the cloth, piece by piece, and got a lot of money. So she smartened up the house and became so grand in her old days that she might have been a great dame. They were both happy and comfortable, but at last that money also came to an end, and one day when the woman had no more food in the house, she said to her son that he would now really have to go to work to make himself useful, else it would come to starvation with both of them.

But the lad thought it would be better to go to old Mother Corner's and woo her daughter. The woman thought the same, for the lad had now fine, new clothes and looked so well that she thought it quite impossible such a fine lad should get "no."

So she dressed him and tidied him as well as she could and he brought out his new boots and polished them till he could see himself in them, and after that he set out.

This time he did not take the shortest cut but went a long way round, for he did not want to get down to the rat any more, he was so tired of all the widdling-waddling and the eternal talk about the wedding. The weather and the roads were just the

"THE ROAD IS A LITTLE NARROW HERE, SO YOU HAD BETTER WALK BY THE SIDE OF THE CARRIAGE, MY DEAR," SAID THE RAT TO THE LAD

same as on the first and second occasion. The sun shone and the water glistened in the puddles and the lad ran and sang, as he always did; but as he was running and jumping along he found himself all at once on the same bridge on the moor again. From this he jumped across a puddle on to a tussock so as not to soil his boots—plump! and down the lad went and he did not stop till he found himself in the same nasty, dark hole again. At first he was glad, for he did not see anything, but when he had been there awhile he caught a glimpse of the ugly rat—the nasty thing —with a bunch of keys on her tail.

"Good-day, my dear!" said the rat; "welcome again! I see you cannot live long without me! I'm glad of that! But everything is now ready for the wedding and we will set out for church at once."

We'll see about that, thought the lad, but he said nothing. The rat then gave a squeak and a swarm of rats and mice came rushing in from all corners, and six big rats came harnessed to a frying-pan; two mice got up behind as footmen and two sat in front driving. Some of them got into the pan, while the rat with the bunch of keys took her place in the middle of them. She then said to the lad:

"The road is a little narrow here, so you had better walk by the side of the carriage, my dear, till the road becomes wider, and then you can sit up beside me."

"How grand we want to be!" thought the lad. "I only wish I was well out of this, and I would run away from the whole crew," he thought; but he said nothing. He followed as best he could. Sometimes he had to creep and sometimes he had to stoop, for the passage was often very low and narrow; but when it became broader he went on in front and looked around to see how he could best manage to give them the slip.

All at once he heard a clear and beautiful voice behind him:

"Now the road is good! Come, my dear, and get into the carriage!"

The lad turned quickly round and nearly lost his wits, for

there stood the most splendid carriage with six white horses; and in the carriage sat a maiden as fair and beautiful as the sun, and around her sat other damsels as handsome and bright as the stars. It was a princess and her playmates who had been enchanted. But now they were freed, because he had gone down to them and never gainsaid them in anything.

"Come now," said the princess, and the lad then stepped into the carriage and drove to church with her. On their way from church the princess said:

"We will now drive to my place first and then we will send for your mother."

"That was all very well," thought the lad; he said nothing this time either, but he thought it would be better to go home to his mother than down in the nasty rat-hole. But all at once they came to a grand castle, where they drove in; and that was their home. A splendid carriage with six horses was then sent to fetch the lad's mother, and when it came back the wedding festivities began. They lasted fourteen days, and perhaps they are still going on. If we make haste we may also be in time to drink with the bridegroom and to dance with the bride.

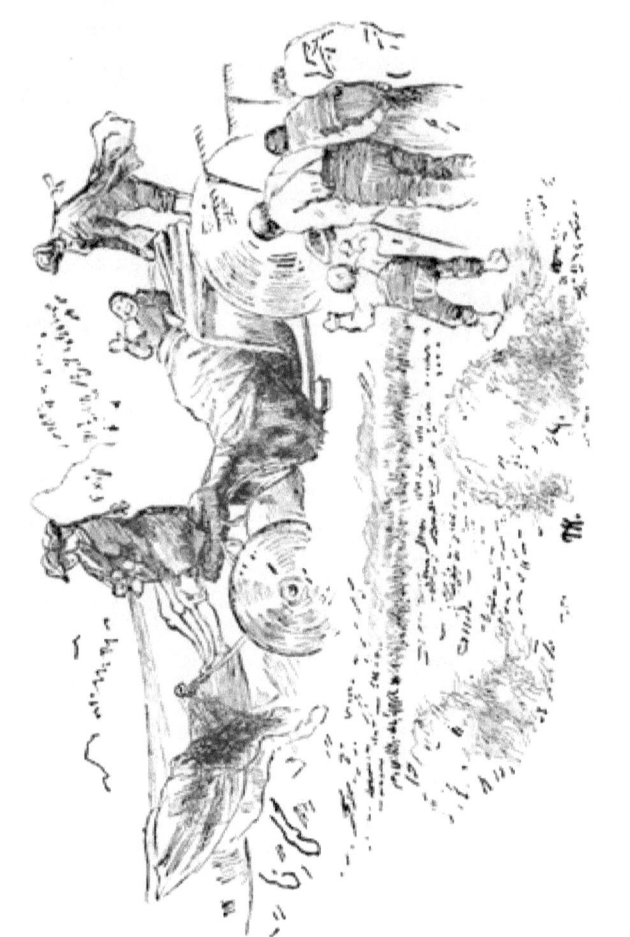

A SPLENDID CARRIAGE WAS SENT TO FETCH THE LAD'S MOTHER

THE PRINCESS WHOM NOBODY COULD SILENCE

There was once upon a time a king, and he had a daughter who would always have the last word; she was so perverse and contrary in her speech that no one could silence her. So the king therefore promised that he who could outwit her should have the princess in marriage and half the kingdom besides. There were plenty of those who wanted to try, I can assure you; for it isn't every day that a princess and half a kingdom are to be had.

The gate to the palace hardly ever stood still. The suitors came in swarms and flocks from east and west, both riding and walking. But there was no one who could silence the princess. At last the king announced that those who tried and did not succeed should be branded on both ears with a large iron; he would not have all this running about the palace for nothing.

So there were three brothers who had also heard about the princess, and as they were rather badly off at home, they thought they would try their luck and see if they could win the princess and half the kingdom. They were good friends and so they agreed to set out together.

When they had got a bit on the way, Ashiepattle found a dead magpie.

"I have found something! I have found something!" cried he.

"What have you found?" asked the brothers.

"I have found a dead magpie," said he.

"Faugh! throw it away; what can you do with that?" said the other two, who always believed they were the wisest.

"Oh, I've nothing else to do. I can easily carry it," said Ashiepattle.

When they had gone on a bit further Ashiepattle found an old willow-twig, which he picked up.

"I have found something! I have found something!" he cried.

"What have you found now?" said the brothers.

"I have found a willow-twig," said he.

"Pooh! what are you going to do with that? Throw it away." said the two.

"I have nothing else to do, I can easily carry it with me," said Ashiepattle.

When they had gone still further he found a broken saucer, which he also picked up.

"Here lads, I have found something! I have found something!" said he.

"Well, what have you found now?" asked the brothers.

"A broken saucer," said he.

"Pshaw! Is it worth while dragging that along with you too? Throw it away!" said the brothers.

"Oh, I've nothing else to do, I can easily carry it with me," said Ashiepattle.

When they had gone a little bit further he found a crooked goat-horn and soon after he found the fellow to it.

"I have found something! I have found something, lads!" said he.

"What have you found now?" said the others.

"Two goat-horns," answered Ashiepattle.

"Ugh! Throw them away! What are you going to do with them?" said they.

"Oh, I have nothing else to do. I can easily carry them with me," said Ashiepattle.

In a little while he found a wedge.

"I say, lads, I have found something! I have found something!" he cried.

"You are everlastingly finding something! What have you found now?" asked the two eldest.

"I have found a wedge," he answered.

"Oh, throw it away! What are you going to do with it?" said they.

"Oh, I have nothing else to do. I can easily carry it with me," said Ashiepattle.

As he went across the king's fields, which had been freshly manured, he stooped down and took up an old boot-sole.

"Hullo, lads! I have found something, I have found something!" said he.

"Heaven grant you may find a little sense before you get to the palace!" said the two. "What is it you have found now?"

"An old boot-sole," said he.

"Is that anything worth picking up? Throw it away! What are you going to do with it?" said the brothers.

"Oh, I have nothing else to do. I can easily carry it with me, and—who knows?—it may help me to win the princess and half the kingdom," said Ashiepattle.

"Yes, you look a likely one, don't you?" said the other two. So they went in to the princess, the eldest first.

"Good day!" said he.

"Good day to you!" answered she, with a shrug.

"It's terribly hot here," said he.

"It's hotter in the fire," said the princess. The branding iron was lying waiting in the fire.

When he saw this he was struck speechless, and so it was all over with him.

The second brother fared no better.

"Good day!" said he.

"Good day to you," said she, with a wriggle.

"It's terribly hot here!" said he.

"It's hotter in the fire," said she. With that he lost both speech and wits, and so the iron had to be brought out.

Then came Ashiepattle's turn.

"Good day!" said he.

"Good day to you!" said she, with a shrug and a wriggle.

"It is very nice and warm here!" said Ashiepattle.

"It's warmer in the fire," she answered. She was in no better humour now she saw the third suitor.

"Then there's a chance for me to roast my magpie on it," said he, bringing it out.

"I'm afraid it will sputter," said the princess.

"No fear of that! I'll tie this willow-twig round it," said the lad.

"You can't tie it tight enough," said she.

"Then I'll drive in a wedge," said the lad, and brought out the wedge.

"The fat will be running off it," said the princess.

"Then I'll hold this under it," said the lad, and showed her the broken saucer.

"You are so crooked in your speech," said the princess.

"No, I am not crooked," answered the lad; "but this is crooked;" and he brought out one of the goat-horns.

"Well, I've never seen the like!" cried the princess.

"Here you see the like," said he, and brought out the other horn.

"It seems you have come here to wear out my soul!" she said.

"No, I have not come here to wear out your soul, for I have one here which is already worn-out," answered the lad, and brought out the old boot-sole.

The princess was so dumbfounded at this, that she was completely silenced.

"Now you are mine!" said Ashiepattle, and so he got her and half the kingdom into the bargain.

"NO, I HAVE NOT COME HERE TO WEAR OUT YOUR SOUL, FOR I HAVE ONE HERE WHICH IS ALREADY WORN OUT," SAID THE LAD, AND BROUGHT OUT THE OLD FOOT-SOLE

FARMER WEATHERBEARD

There were once upon a time a man and a woman, who had an only son, and he was called Hans. The woman thought that he ought to go out and look for work, and told her husband to go with him. "You must find him such a good place, that he can become master of all masters," she said, and so she put some food and a roll of tobacco in a bag for them.

Well, they went to many masters, but all replied that they might make the lad as clever as they were themselves, but they could not make him cleverer. When the man came home to his wife with this answer, she said: "Well, I don't care what you do with him, but this I tell you, that you will have to make him master over all masters." So she put some food and a roll of tobacco in a bag, and the man and the son had to set out again.

When they had gone a bit on the way, they came out upon the ice, where they met a man who was driving a black horse.

"Where are you going?" said he.

"I'm going to get my son apprenticed to some one who can teach him well; for my wife comes of such good people, that she wants him to become master of all masters."

"That's lucky," said the man who was driving; "I am the

very man for that, and I am just looking for such an apprentice. Get up behind," he said to the boy, and off they went through the air.

"Wait a bit!" shouted the lad's father. "I ought to know what's your name and where you live?" said he.

"Oh, I'm at home both North and South and East and West, and I am called Farmer Weatherbeard," said the master. "In a year you can come back again, and I will tell you if he's good for anything." And off they went, and were lost to sight.

When the year was out, the man came to hear about his son. "You can't finish him in a year, you know," said the master. "As yet he has only found his legs, so to speak." They then agreed that Farmer Weatherbeard should keep him another year, and teach him everything, and then the man was to come back for him. When the year was over they met again at the same place.

"Have you finished with him now?" asked the father.

"Yes, he's my master now, but you will never see him again," said Farmer Weatherbeard; and before the man knew what had become of them, they were gone, both the farmer and the lad.

When the man came home, the woman asked if the son was not with him, or what had become of him.

"Oh, goodness knows what became of him," said the man; "he went off through the air." And so he told her what had happened. When the woman heard that her husband did not know where her son was, she sent him off again.

"You must find the lad, even if you have to go to Old Nick for him!" said she, and gave him a bag of food and a roll of tobacco.

"When he had got a bit on the way, he came to a large forest, and it took him the whole of the day to get through it; and as it grew dark he saw a bright light and went towards it. After a long while he came to a little cottage under a cliff, and outside it a woman was standing, drawing water from the well with her nose, it was so long.

THE WOMAN WAS RAKING THE FIRE WITH HER NOSE, IT WAS SO LONG

"Good evening, mother!"

"Good evening to you," said the woman; "no one has called me mother for a hundred years."

"Can I get lodgings here to-night?" said the man.

"No," said the woman. But then the man brought out the roll of tobacco, dried a little of it and made some snuff, which he gave the woman. She was so glad that she began to dance, and then she said that he might stop the night.

All at once he asked after Farmer Weatherbeard. She knew nothing about him, she said, but she ruled over all four-footed animals, and perhaps some of them might know something about him. She then called them together with a whistle, and questioned them, but there was not one who knew anything about Farmer Weatherbeard.

"Well, we are three sisters," said the woman; "perhaps one of the other two knows where he is. I'll lend you my carriage so that you can get there to-night, but it is three hundred miles to the nearest of them."

The man set out and got there in the evening. When he arrived, there also was a woman standing drawing water from the well with her nose.

"Good evening, mother!" said the man.

"Good evening to you," said the woman; "no one has called me mother for a hundred years," said she.

"Can I get lodgings here to-night?" said the man.

"No," said the woman.

But then the man brought out the roll of tobacco, dried a little of it and made some snuff, which he gave the woman on the back of her hand. She was so pleased at this that she began to dance, and then she said he might stop there the night.

All at once he asked about Farmer Weatherbeard. She did not know anything about him, but she ruled over all the fishes, she said, and perhaps some of them might know something about him. She then called them together with a whistle she had, and questioned them all, but there was not one who knew anything about Farmer Weatherbeard.

"Well, I have another sister; perhaps she may know something about him; she lives six hundred miles from here, but you can have my carriage and get there before night sets in."

The man set out and got there in the evening, and found a woman raking the fire with her nose, it was so long.

"Good evening, mother!"

"Good evening to you," said the woman; "no one has called me mother for a hundred years."

"Can I get lodgings here to-night?" said the man.

"No," said the woman.

But then the man brought out the tobacco roll again and began to make some snuff. He gave the woman so much that it covered the whole of the back of her hand. She was so pleased at this that she began to dance, and then she said he might stop the night.

All at once he asked about Farmer Weatherbeard. She did not know anything about him, she said; but she ruled over all the birds and called them all together with her whistle. When she had questioned them all, she missed the eagle, but in a little while he came; and when she asked him, he said he had come straight from Farmer Weatherbeard. The woman then told him that he must show the man the way there. But first the eagle wanted something to eat, and next he wanted to rest till the following day, for he was so tired after the long way he had come, that he could scarcely rise from the ground.

When the eagle had finished his meal and taken a rest, the woman plucked a feather from his tail and put the man in its place, and away flew the eagle with him; but they did not get to Farmer Weatherbeard before midnight. When they arrived there, the eagle said:

"There are bones and carcases lying about outside the door, but you must not mind them. All the people in the house sleep so soundly that they are hard to wake; you must go straight to the

THE MAN DID AS HE WAS TOLD AND PULLED A FEATHER OUT OF FARMER WEATHERBEARD'S HEAD

table drawer and take three bits of bread out of it, and if you hear some one snoring you must pull three feathers out of his head; that won't wake him up."

The man did as he was told, and when he had got the bits of bread, he pulled out first one feather.

"Oh!" cried Farmer Weatherbeard.

Then the man pulled out one more and Farmer Weatherbeard shouted "Oh" again; but when he pulled out the third one, Farmer Weatherbeard shrieked so loudly that the man thought both the walls and the roof would have burst asunder, but the farmer went on sleeping just the same. The eagle then told the man what he was to do next; so he went to the door of the cow-house, and there he stumbled against a big stone, which he took with him, and under the stone lay three chips of wood, which he also took with him. He then knocked at the door of the cow-house and it opened at once. He dropped the three bits of bread, and a hare came running out and ate them. He then caught the hare and took it with him.

The eagle asked him to pluck three feathers out of his tail and place the hare, the stone, the chips of wood and himself instead, and he would then fly home with them. When the eagle had flown a long, long away, he settled down on a stone.

"Do you see anything?" said he.

"Yes, I see a flock of crows flying towards us," said the man.

"We had better get on a bit then," said the eagle, and on he flew. In a while he asked again:

"Do you see anything now?"

"Yes, the crows are close upon us again," said the man.

"Drop the three feathers you plucked from his head," said the eagle.

The man did so, and the moment he dropped them the feathers became a flock of ravens, which chased the crows home again. The eagle then flew far away with the man. At last it settled down on a stone to rest.

"Do you see anything?" he said.

"I'm not sure," said the man, "but I think I see something coming far away."

"We had better get on a bit then," said the eagle.

"Do you see anything now?" he said in a while.

"Yes, now he is close upon us," said the man.

"You must drop the chips which you took from under the stone near the cow-house door," said the eagle.

The man did so, and the same moment he dropped them there grew up a great, thick forest; so Farmer Weatherbeard had to go home for axes to cut his way through.

The eagle then flew on again a long way, till he became tired and settled down in a fir-tree.

"Do you see anything?" said he.

"Well, I'm not sure about it," said the man, "but I think I catch a glimpse of something far away."

"We had better get on a bit then," said the eagle; and so he flew on again.

"Do you see anything now?" he said in a while.

"Yes, now he is close upon us."

"You must drop the stone you took from the cow-house door," said the eagle.

The man did so, and it became a big, lofty mountain, which Farmer Weatherbeard had to break his way through. But when he had got half-way through the mountain he broke one of his legs, so that he had to go home and get it healed.

In the meantime the eagle flew home with the man and the hare, and when they got there the man went to the churchyard and put some consecrated soil on the hare, and it changed into Hans, his own son.

When the time came round for the fair, the lad turned himself into a cream-coloured horse, and asked his father to take him with him to the fair.

"If some one comes up to you and wants to buy me, you must say you want a hundred dollars for me; but you must not forget to take off the halter, otherwise I shall never be able to get away

"YOU MUST DROP THE STONE YOU TOOK FROM THE COW-HOUSE DOOR," SAID THE EAGLE

from Farmer Weatherbeard; for it is he who will come and want to buy me," said the lad.

And so it turned out. A horse-dealer came up and wanted to buy the horse, and the man got his hundred dollars for it. But when the bargain was made, and Hans's father had got the money, the horse-dealer wanted to keep the halter also.

"No, there was nothing about that in our agreement," said the man. "You cannot have the halter, for I have more horses to bring to town."

So they went each his way. But they had not got far before Hans resumed his own shape, and when the man came home he found the son sitting by the stove.

The second day he turned himself into a brown horse, and told his father to take him with him to the fair.

"If some one comes up to you and wants to buy me, you must say you want two hundred dollars for me; for he will pay you that and give you a drink besides; but whatever you drink or whatever you do, you must not forget to take the halter off me, else you will not see me again," said Hans.

It turned out just as before. The man got two hundred dollars for the horse, and a drink into the bargain; and when they parted, it was as much as the man could do to remember to take off the halter. But they had not got far on the road before the lad resumed his own shape, and when the man came home Hans was already sitting by the stove.

The third day the same thing happened again. The lad turned himself into a big, black horse and told his father that some one would come up to him and offer him three hundred dollars and treat him freely to drink; but whatever he did or however much he drank he must not forget to take off the halter, otherwise he would never get away from Farmer Weatherbeard in his life.

No, he would not forget that, said the man. When he came to the fair he got the three hundred dollars, but Farmer Weatherbeard treated him to so much drink that he forgot to take off the halter and Farmer Weatherbeard set off with the horse.

When he had got a bit on the way he went into a place to get some more drink, and so he put a barrel of red hot nails under the horse's nose and a trough of oats under his tail, hung the halter across a hurdle and went in to the innkeeper. The horse stood there stamping and kicking and snorting and scenting the air. A girl then came by, who took pity on him.

"Poor creature! What sort of a master have you got, who can treat you in this way?" said she, and pushed the halter off the hurdle so that the horse could turn round and eat the oats.

"I am his master!" shouted Farmer Weatherbeard, who came rushing out through the door. But the horse had already shaken off the halter and thrown himself into the horse pond, where he changed himself into a little fish.

Farmer Weatherbeard rushed after him and changed himself into a big pike. Hans then turned himself into a pigeon and Farmer Weatherbeard changed into a hawk and set off after the pigeon. At that moment a princess was standing at a window in the palace and watched this struggle.

"If you knew as much as I do you would come in through the window to me," said the princess to the pigeon.

The pigeon flew in through the window and then changed into Hans, who told her what had happened.

"Change yourself into a gold ring and put yourself on my finger," said she.

"No, that is no use," said Hans, "for Farmer Weatherbeard will then make the king ill; and there is no one who can make him well till Farmer Weatherbeard comes to cure him, and he will ask for the gold ring as payment."

"I will say it is my mother's and that I will not part with it for anything," said the princess.

So Hans changed himself into a gold ring and placed himself on the princess's finger and there Farmer Weatherbeard could not get hold of him.

But it happened just as the lad had said. The king became ill and there was no doctor who could cure him till Farmer Weatherbeard came, and he wanted the ring on the princess's finger for his fee.

The king then sent to the princess for the ring, but she would not part with it, she said, for it had been left her by her mother. When the king heard this he became angry and said he would have the ring, no matter who had left it her.

"Well, it is no use getting angry," said the princess, "for I cannot get it off my finger. If you want the ring you must take the finger as well."

"I will help you and I shall soon get the ring off," said Farmer Weatherbeard.

"No, thank you! I will try myself," said the princess and went to the hearth and put some ashes on it. The ring then slipped off and was lost in the ashes.

Farmer Weatherbeard then turned himself into a cock, which scratched and rooted about in the hearth after the ring so that the ashes flew about their ears. But Hans changed into a fox and bit the cock's head off, and if the evil one was in Farmer Weatherbeard, it was now all over with him.

Printed by BALLANTYNE HANSON & Co.
London & Edinburgh.

MR. DAVID NUTT'S LIST OF

GIFT-BOOKS FOR CHILDREN OF ALL AGES, *for the most part fully illustrated by leading artists in black and white, sumptuously printed on specially made paper, bound in attractive and original covers, and sold at the lowest price consistent with equitable remuneration to authors and artists, and beauty and durability of get up.*

CONTENTS.

FAIRY TALES OF THE BRITISH EMPIRE.
WORKS BY HIS HONOUR JUDGE E. A. PARRY.
WORKS BY MRS. RADFORD.
WORKS ILLUSTRATED BY MISS WINIFRED SMITH.
WORKS BY MRS. LEIGHTON, ASBJÖRNSEN, ETC.

All works in the present list may be had post free from the Publisher at the annexed prices, and are kept on sale by the leading booksellers of the United Kingdom.

"The Ideal Gift-Books of the Season."

FAIRY TALES OF THE BRITISH EMPIRE.

Collected and Edited by JOSEPH JACOBS.

Illustrated by J. D. BATTEN.

MR. JACOBS' FAIRY TALES, which have been appearing since 1890, have won immediate and widespread acceptance. The choice of matter, the simplicity and suitable character of the language of the text, the beauty, humour, and charm of Mr. BATTEN'S Illustrations, and the large and legible type, have commended the series alike to children and to lovers of art; whilst the prefaces and elaborate notes, parallels, and references added by the Editor, have made them indispensable to the increasingly large portion of the public interested in the history and archæology of popular fiction.

"Fairy Tales of the British Empire" are to be had in two forms, at 3s. 6d. and at 6s. a volume.

In so far as Tales and Illustrations are concerned, the 3s. 6d. Edition will be the same as the original 6s. one. But the Editor's Prefaces, Notes, Parallels, and References are omitted.

A full list of the Series, a specimen of Mr. BATTEN'S beautiful Illustrations, and a very small selection from the numberless kindly notices which the Press has bestowed upon the Series, will be found on the following pages.

Fairy Tales of the British Empire.

English Fairy Tales. *Complete* Edition, xvi., 255 pages. 9 full-page Plates, and numerous Illustrations in the text. Designed Cloth Cover, Uncut or Gilt Edges. **6s.**

The same. *Children's* Edition, viii., 227 pages, 7 full-page Plates, and numerous Illustrations in text. Cloth, Cut. **3s. 6d.**

More English Fairy Tales. *Complete* Edition, xvi., 243 pages. 8 full-page, and numerous Illustrations in text. Designed Cloth Cover, Uncut or Gilt Edges. **6s.**

The same. *Children's* Edition, viii., 214 pages, 7 full-page Plates, and numerous Illustrations in text. Cloth, Cut. **3s. 6d.**

Celtic Fairy Tales. *Complete* Edition, xvi., 274 pages. 8 full-page Plates, numerous Illustrations in text. Designed Cloth Cover, Uncut or Gilt Edges. **6s.**

The same. *Children's* Edition, viii., 236 pages, 7 full-page Plates and numerous Illustrations in text. Cloth, Cut. **3s. 6d.**

More Celtic Fairy Tales. *Complete* Edition, xvi., 234 pages, 8 full-page Plates, numerous Illustrations in text. Designed Cloth Cover, Uncut or Gilt Edges. **6s.**

The same. *Children's* Edition, viii., 217 pages, 7 full-page Plates, and numerous Illustrations in text. Cloth, Cut. **3s. 6d.**

Indian Fairy Tales. *Complete* Edition, xvi., 255 pages, 9 full-page Plates, and numerous Illustrations in text. Designed Cloth Cover, Uncut or Gilt Edges. **6s.**

No Children's Edition of the "Indian Fairy Tales" will be issued for the present.

N.B.—A few copies of the Japanese Vellum Issues, printed in large 8vo, with double state of the plates, are still to be had of Indian, More Celtic, and More English Fairy Tales. Prices may be learnt on application to the Publisher. The special issues of English and Celtic Fairy Tales, entirely out of print, command a heavy premium.

Specimen of Mr. Batten's full-page Illustrations to "Fairy Tales of the British Empire."

Some Press Notices

OF

JACOBS' AND BATTEN'S FAIRY TALES.

English Fairy Tales.

Daily Graphic.—"As a collection of fairy tales to delight children of all ages, ranks second to none." *Globe.*—"A delight alike to the young people and their elders." *England.*—"A most delightful volume of fairy tales." *Daily News.*—"A more desirable child's book . . . has not been seen for many a day." *Athenæum.*—"From first to last, almost without exception, these stories are delightful." E. S. HARTLAND.—"The most delightful book of fairy tales, taking form and contents together, ever presented to children." Miss THACKERAY.—"This delightful book." *Review of Reviews.*—"Nothing could be more fascinating."

Celtic Fairy Tales.

Scotsman.—"One of the best books of stories ever put together." *Freeman's Journal.*—"An admirable selection." *Ariel.*—"Delightful stories, exquisite illustrations by John D. Batten, and learned notes." *Daily Telegraph.*—"A stock of delightful little narratives." *Daily Chronicle.*—"A charming volume skilfully illustrated." *Pall Mall Budget.*—"A perfectly lovely book. And oh! the wonderful pictures inside." *Liverpool Daily Post.*—"The best fairy book of the present season." *Oban Times.*—"Many a mother will bless Mr. Jacobs, and many a door will be open to him from Land's End to John o' Groat's."

More English Fairy Tales.

Athenæum.—"Will become more popular with children than its predecessor." *Notes and Queries.*—"Delightful and in every respect worthy of its predecessor." *Glasgow Herald.*—"A more delightful collection of fairy tales could hardly be wished for." *Glasgow Evening News.*—"The new volume of 'English Fairy Tales' is worthy of the one that went before, and this is really saying a great deal."

More Celtic Fairy Tales.

Daily Chronicle.—"A bright exemplar of almost all a fairy-tale book should be." *Saturday Review.*—"Delightful for reading and profitable for comparison." *Notes and Queries.*—"A delightful companion into a land of enchantment." *Irish Daily Independent.*—"Full of bold and beautiful illustrations." *North British Daily Mail.*—"The stories are admirable, and nothing could be better in their way than the designs." *News of the World.*—"Mr. Batten has a real genius for depicting fairy folk."

Indian Fairy Tales.

Dublin Daily Express.—"Unique and charming anthology." *Daily News.*—"Good for the schoolroom and the study." *Star.*—"Illustrated with a charming freshness of fancy." *Gloucester Journal.*—"A book which is something more than a valuable addition to folk-lore; a book for the student as well as for the child." *Scotsman.*—"Likely to prove a perfect success." *Literary World.*—"Admirably grouped, and very enjoyable."

WORKS BY HIS HONOUR
JUDGE EDWARD ABBOTT PARRY.

Illustrated by ARCHIE MACGREGOR.

THE issue of *Katawampus: its Treatment and Cure*, in the Christmas Season of 1895, revealed a writer for children who, in originality, spontaneity, and fulness of humour as well as in sympathy with and knowledge of childhood, may be compared, and not to his disadvantage, with Lewis Carroll. And, as is the case with "Alice in Wonderland," an illustrator was found whose sympathy with his author and capacity for rendering his conceptions have won immediate and widespread recognition. A specimen of the illustrations and a small selection from the press notices will be found overleaf.

KATAWAMPUS: its Treatment and Cure. Second Edition. 96 pages, Cloth. **3s. 6d.**

BUTTER-SCOTIA, or, a Cheap Trip to Fairy Land. 180 pages. Map of Butter-Scotia, many Full-page Plates and Illustrations in the Text. Bound in specially designed Cloth Cover. **6s.**

KATAWAMPUS KANTICLES. Music by Sir J. F. BRIDGE, Mus. Doc., Organist of Westminster Abbey. Words by His Honour Judge E. A. PARRY. Illustrated Cover, representing Kapellmeister Krab, by ARCHIE MACGREGOR. Royal 8vo, **1s.**

For Christmas 1897.

THE FIRST BOOK OF KRAB. Christmas Stories for Children of all Ages. 132 pages, with many Full-page Plates and Illustrations in the Text. Bound in specially designed Cloth Cover. **3s. 6d.**

KATAWAMPUS: Its Treatment and Cure.

By His Honour Judge E. A. PARRY.

Illustrated by ARCHIE MACGREGOR.

Second Edition, Cloth, 3s. 6d.

Press Notices.

"One of the very best books of the season." *The World.*

"A very delightful and original book." *Review of Reviews.*

"The book is one of rare drollery, and the verses and pictures are capital of their kind."—*Saturday Review.*

"We strongly advise both parents and children to read the book."—*Guardian.*

"A truly delightful little book. . . ."—*Pall Mall Gazette.*

"A tale full of jinks and merriment." *Daily Chronicle.*

"The brightest, wittiest, and most logical fairy-tale we have read for a long time."—*Westminster Gazette.*

"Its fun is of the sort that children revel in and 'grown-ups' also relish, so spontaneous and irresistible is it."
Manchester Guardian.

"A delightful extravaganza of the 'Wonderland' type, but by no means a slavish imitation."—*Glasgow Herald.*

"Since 'Alice in Wonderland' there has not been a book more calculated to become a favourite in the nursery."—*Baby.*

GOT HIM THIS TIME

THE BOOK OF WONDER VOYAGES.

Edited with Introduction and Notes by JOSEPH JACOBS.

Illustrated by J. D. BATTEN.

Square demy 8vo, sumptuously printed in large clear type on specially manufactured paper, at the Ballantyne Press. With Photogravure Frontispiece, and many Full-page Illustrations and Designs in the Text. Specially designed Cloth Cover, 6s.

Contents.—The Argonauts—The Voyage of Maelduin—The Journeyings of Hasan of Bassorah to the Islands of Wak-Wak—How Thorkill went to the Under World and Eric the Far-Travelled to Paradise.

This, the latest of the volumes in which Mr. Jacobs and Mr. Batten have collaborated with such admirable results, will be welcomed as heartily as its predecessors by the children of the English-speaking world. A specimen of Mr. Batten's illustration is appended.

WORKS ILLUSTRATED BY MISS WINIFRED SMITH, Silver and Gold Medallist, South Kensington, Winner of the Princess of Wales' Prize, etc. etc.

CHILDREN'S SINGING GAMES, with the Tunes

to which they are Sung. Collected and Edited by ALICE BERTHA GOMME. Pictured in Black and White by WINIFRED SMITH. Two Series, each 3s. 6d.

Charming albums in small oblong 4to, printed on antique paper and bound in specially designed cloth cover, and serving equally for the nursery, the schoolroom, and the drawing-room. Mrs. Gomme, the first living authority on English games, has carefully chosen the finest and most interesting of the old traditional singing games, has provided accurate text and music, has given precise directions for playing, and added notes pointing out the historical interests of these survivals of old world practices. The humour, spirit, and grace of Miss Winifred Smith's drawings may be sufficiently gauged from the annexed specimens and from the following press notices.

Some Press Notices of "Children's Singing Games."

Baby.—"A delightful gift for little boys and girls. . . . Cannot fail to become quickly popular."

Journal of Education.—"Most charmingly illustrated."

Saturday Review.—"A truly fascinating book. . . . It is hopeless to make a choice which is best. The traditional rhymes and music, so quaintly and prettily illustrated, with moreover so much humour and go in all the designs, are charming."

Scotsman.—"The pictures must please anybody who can appreciate delicate humour."

Bookman.—"The designs are witty, pretty, and effective."

Sylvia's Journal.—"The illustrations are charming."

NURSERY SONGS AND RHYMES OF ENGLAND.

Pictured in Black and White by WINIFRED SMITH. Small 4to. Printed on hand-made paper. In specially designed cloth cover, 3s. 6d.

Some Press Notices of "Nursery Songs and Rhymes."

Literary World.—"Delightfully illustrated."

Athenæum.—"Very cleverly drawn and humorous designs."

Manchester Guardian.—"All the designs are very apt and suited to the comprehension of a child."

Scotsman.—"The designs are full of grace and fun, and give the book an artistic value not common in nursery literature."

Globe.—"The drawings are distinctly amusing and sure to delight children."

Star.—"Really a beautiful book. . . . Winifred Smith has revelled into old rhymes, and young and old alike will in their turn revel in the results of her artistic revelry."

Pall Mall Gazette.—"No book of nursery rhymes has charmed us so much."

Magazine of Art.—"Quite a good book of its kind."

Woman.—"Miss Smith's drawings are now celebrated and are indeed very beautiful, decorative, and full of naive humour."

WORKS BY MRS. ERNEST RADFORD.

SONGS FOR SOMEBODY. Verses by DOLLIE RADFORD. Pictures by GERTRUDE BRADLEY. Square crown 8vo. Six plates printed in colour by EDMUND EVANS, and 36 designs in monochrome. Coloured cover by LOUIS DAVIS. 3s. 6d.

GOOD NIGHT. Verses by DOLLIE RADFORD. Designs by LOUIS DAVIS. Forty pages entirely designed by the artist and pulled on the finest and the thickest cartridge paper. Boards and canvas back with label, 2s. 6d.

Some Press Notices.

Daily Chronicle.—" As far as we know no one else sings quite like Mrs. Radford; hers is a bird's note—thin, high, with a sweet thrill in it, and the thrill is a home thrill, a nest thrill."

Commonwealth.—" We have read with pure enjoyment Mrs. Radford's slight but charming cycle of rhymes."

Star.—" A tender spirit of motherhood inspires Mrs. Radford's simple little songs."

Review of Reviews.—" Very charming poems for children not unworthy even to be mentioned in the same breath with Stevenson's 'Child's Garden of Verses.'"

Athenæum.—"'Good Night' is one of the daintiest little books we have seen for years. The verses are graceful and pretty, and the illustrations excellent. It will please both young and old."

Literary World.—" Charming little songs of childhood."

New Age.—" Mrs. Radford is closely in touch with a child's mind, and her ideal child is a nice, soft, loving little creature whom we all want to caress in our arms."

Artist.—" Since Blake died never has a book been produced which can so truly be described as a labour of love to the artist as 'Good Night.'"

MEDIÆVAL LEGENDS. Being a Gift-Book to the Children of England, of Five Old-World Tales from France and Germany. Demy 8vo. Designed cloth cover, 3s. 6d.

Contents.—The Mysterious History of Melusina—The Story of Æsop—The Rhyme of the Seven Swabians—The Sweet and Touching Tale of Fleur and Blanchefleur—The Wanderings of Duke Ernest.

Some Press Notices.

Saturday Review.—" A capital selection of famous legends."

Times.—" There can be no question as to the value of this gift."

Morning Post.—" Full of romantic incident, of perilous adventure by land and sea."

Guardian.—" This delightful volume. . . . In all respects admirable."

World.—" An elegant and tasteful volume."

THE HAPPY PRINCE, and other Tales. By OSCAR WILDE. 116 pages, small 4to. Beautifully printed in old-faced type, on cream-laid paper, with wide margins. Bound in Japanese vellum cover, printed in red and black. With three full-page Plates by WALTER CRANE, and eleven Vignettes by JACOMB HOOD. Second Edition. 3s. 6d.

Some Press Notices.

Christian Leader.—"Beautiful exceedingly; charmingly devised—exquisitely told."

Universal Review.—"Heartily recommended."

Athenæum.—"Mr. Wilde possesses the gift of writing fairy tales in a rare degree."

Dublin Evening Mail.—"A beautiful book in every sense."

Glasgow Herald.—"It is difficult to speak too highly of these tales."

For Christmas 1897.

FAIRY TALES FROM THE FAR NORTH. By P. C. ASBJÖRNSEN. Translated by H. L. BRÆKSTAD. With 94 Illustrations by E. WERENSKIOLD, T. KITTELSEN, and H. SINDING. Small 4to ("Wonder Voyages" size), beautifully printed at the Ballantyne Press on specially manufactured paper. Cloth, designed Cover. **6s.**

⁎⁎⁎ The raciest and quaintest of stories, the most spirited and humorous of illustrations.

THE GIANT CRAB, and other Tales from Old India. Retold by W. H. D. ROUSE. Profusely Illustrated by W. ROBINSON. Square crown 8vo, beautifully printed at the Ballantyne Press on special paper. Designed cloth cover. **3s. 6d.**

⁎⁎⁎ Adaptation for English children of Tales from the Oldest Story Book in the world, the Jatakas, or Birth-stories of Buddha.

www.ingramcontent.com/pod-product-compliance
Lightning Source LLC
Chambersburg PA
CBHW030807230426
43667CB00008B/1098